Rituals For Living
Dreambook + Planner

Please visit **www.dreambook.vision** for more details, exercises, and valuable resources.

Hang With Us

/thedragontree

@dragontreespa

@thedragontree

thedragontree.com

Third Edition © 2016 by Peter Borten and Briana Borten. All rights reserved.
No reproduction, alteration, duplication, or transmission without author permission, please.
ISBN 978-0-9967278-6-0

Welcome From Our Founders

Now is the time to take the first steps toward actualizing your dreams while simultaneously prioritizing your health and happiness. We're so happy to be part of this journey with you, and we firmly believe that if you set out to achieve your goals while remaining steadfast on the necessity of playing, caring for yourself, connecting to family, friends, a higher power, and the natural world – you actually amplify your ability to succeed.

We believe in you and we're honored to help in getting your genius out into the world.

Love,

Briana & Peter

Ritual Makes the Difference

Want to live a meaningful life?

Many of us want to feel a greater sense of meaning and purpose in our lives, but aren't sure where this would come from. The secret is that *we* are in charge of creating the meaning and purpose.

Historically, we had rituals for everything that mattered. But ritual is gradually disappearing as people find they're too busy for it or can't see the value in it. Even a ritual as simple as enjoying the peace of the new morning is so often sacrificed for whatever new alerts our phone might have for us. There's more depression and anxiety than ever before, more uncertainty about where we fit in, and yet, the opportunity to reconnect is always available.

Ritual brings order, specialness, context and focus to our lives. The opening and closing, or the initiation and conclusion of a ritual aligns our intention with our actions, and it sets the stage for the action to be as effective as possible. Ritual grounds us in the present; it rescues us from dwelling on the past and worrying about the future.

You probably already have some rituals – like brewing a cup of coffee and sitting down to plan your day. We believe it's worth bringing more awareness to these rituals, and consciously forging new ones, even if their value is entirely subjective. Your experience of your day and your life will have a structure and specialness that's meaningful to *you*. Wouldn't it be worth it?

You *will* see objective change, too. As you implement healthy rituals, your outlook will change, your beliefs may change, and the world you create around yourself will change. Don't just dream and set goals, ritualize their actualization.

How This Book Works

CONNECT

We start by connecting with what's really important to you. This section is designed to help you identify your core values, your gifts, and your life purpose.

DREAM

This is the space to stretch your imagination around what you might think is possible. Stop playing small and start seeing yourself as the magical creator that you are. You can create anything you want. We want to help ensure that what you're creating reflects your highest potential and most authentic self.

CRAFT

This is where it gets real. You'll be selecting items from the Dream section to pursue, and you'll create mind maps to flesh them out.

RITUALIZE

Next, it's time to come up with the rituals that will make this process fun, meaningful, and an integral part of your life.

PLAN

Yearly, quarterly, monthly, and weekly planning is essential to keep you on track with your big dreams, your happiness, and your health.

Create Space for What's Most Important

Why the arrows? The arrow theme is a reminder of the incredible power of your attention. It's easy to get distracted from what's important by what feels urgent in the moment, by every new email, or by a list of mundane tasks that "need" our immediate attention. But we encourage you to treat your attention as a valuable thing – like golden arrows – because your energy flows in the direction of your attention. What you put your attention on grows and becomes a theme of your life – whether you mean for this or not.

We invite you to experience a new way of life where YOU are in charge and you focus your precious energy on what truly matters to you. It's unlikely that anyone gets to the end of life and wishes they had spent more time playing on their phone. As you take your last breaths, what do you want to have done with your life? In the end, only you get to decide if it was a life well lived. You're shaping it right now. If you don't like where you're headed, there's no time like the present to begin changing your course.

With that, we have one big rule for planning:

Schedule what's most important first. Always.

Consider These Six Main Areas of Life

- ⇒ Physical Wellness
- ⇒ Psychological and Spiritual Health
- ⇒ Creation, Exploration, and Play
- ⇒ Community Connection
- ⇒ Livelihood, Career, and Influence
- ⇒ Relationship and Family

Questions to Connect You to Your True Desires and Purpose

Answer these questions honestly. As if no one else will ever see your answers. As if your parents would be thrilled no matter who you are and no matter what you do with your life. As if no one else's opinion matters. These responses are for you alone, so you have everything to gain by reaching deep.

1. What are you longing for most in life?

_____
_____
_____
_____

2. When you're at the end of life what do you want to have accomplished?

_____
_____
_____
_____

3. If you knew you had one year left to live, would there be anything you'd want to fix or clean up?

4. What are you ready to let go of – habits, attitudes, obligations, beliefs, outdated goals, etc. – that is not serving you?

5. What do you want to explore more deeply?

6. What would make life feel ridiculously fun?

7. What feels really nourishing in your life?

8. Of all the things you've done or accomplished in your life, what has given you the deepest sense of fulfillment? When have you been most proud of yourself?

9. Where do you find yourself not being fully "present" in your life, or not participating fully?

Discovering Your Core Values and Gifts

Are you ever faced with a major (or not-so-major) life decision you're uncertain about? Like what to do about a job offer, or a prospective relationship, or a new place to live? We've been there. And we've found that besides a good ol' pros and cons list, it's helpful to have identified your core values. You can reflect on your list to guide you to healthy long term decisions.

For help discovering these values, first look at the answers to your questions in the previous section. Consider your greatest accomplishments and failures. When have you been most productive? When do you like yourself the most? What advice would you give someone based on what you've learned? Look for common themes.

Here are some potential core values to give you ideas from which you can develop and refine your own:

Honesty	Enjoyment	Achievement
Kindness	Flexibility	Lightness
Integrity	Trustworthiness	Learning
Purpose	Beauty	Discipline
Compassion	Courage	Generosity
Love	Wisdom	Devotion
Ambition	Openness	Optimism
Expression	Humility	Respectfulness
Individuality	Simplicity	Vision
Community	Equality	Truthfulness
Service	Righteousness	Persistence

Choose a few values that resonate with you and follow naturally from your previous answers:

_____

_____

_____

Your Gifts

Now, looking again through your previous answers and free writing, what are your talents and gifts? Are you good at helping others to feel heard? Do you have an ability to create art? Are you a gifted communicator? Are you skilled at connecting with children or animals? This is not the time for modesty. Everyone has gifts. Everyone is a healer. Everyone has the capacity to create beauty. Write about your talents and gifts here:

_____

_____

_____

_____

Purpose

Considering your core values and your gifts, what might your life purpose be? "Life purpose" can sound so grand, so out of our hands. Few people have the experience of knowing their purpose and accessing the clarity that comes from it, because we believe it's a revelation that's delivered through some dramatic or mystical experience. Or that sometimes we're just lucky enough to stumble upon a path that we feel a profound sense of conviction about.

The crazy thing is, rather than waiting around to see if we'll be assigned a life purpose, we can just choose one. If you choose with your heart, you'll choose something that's at least in the right direction, and over time you'll refine and evolve it. Don't worry about getting it perfect.

Frame your purpose as a way that you can serve or help. That is, given your values and gifts, how might these be of value to your species? Or to the planet? Or to children? Or to refugees? Or to endangered plants and animals? Or to any other group that could benefit from your unique talents?

Consider how you could work your core values and gifts into a service-oriented statement of purpose. Such as, "My purpose is to help children heal through art." Or, "My purpose is to empower women to learn and use their voices." Or, "My purpose is to help my species survive through communication." Or, "My purpose is to make the world more beautiful." We'll get you started:

My purpose is _____.

Now that you have a clearer sense of your core values, your gifts, and your purpose, it should be easier to get a sense of your priorities. Knowing these "soul drives" can be a valuable guide through difficult experiences and tough decisions.

You can always ask yourself:

{
»→ **IS THIS ALIGNED WITH MY CORE VALUES?**
OR, IF I WERE TO APPROACH THIS WHILE EMBODYING MY CORE VALUES, HOW WOULD I ACT?

»→ **DOES THIS ALLOW ME TO SHARE MY GIFTS?**
OR, IF I HONORED AND UTILIZED MY GIFTS TO MY FULLEST POTENTIAL, HOW WOULD I ACT?

»→ **GIVEN MY LIFE PURPOSE OF ..... IS THIS "ON PURPOSE" FOR ME?**
OR, IF I WERE ACTING IN ACCORDANCE WITH MY LIFE PURPOSE OF ..... HOW WOULD I ACT?
}

Often, this quickly brings you clarity. You may not be successful at always staying aware and reverent of your values, gifts, and purpose, but when you begin to consciously do this more and more, you'll experience a sense of *alignment* – a *knowing* that you're on the right track – and there's both peace and power in this.

Vision of the Future

Imagine your life three years from now and create a positive picture using the questions below. Really feel into exactly what you want. You can have anything - you just have to choose.

Livelihood, Career, Influence

Projecting three years into the future of your wildest dreams, consider these details about how you earn money, the work you do, and the nature of your influence on the world. Answer all the questions from this perspective.

1. What does your business/career look and feel like?

_____
_____
_____
_____

2. How much money do you make? What other benefits do you get?

_____
_____
_____

3. How do you feel when you get up in the morning to start your work day (even if this work isn't how you earn money)?

_____
_____
_____
_____

4. What do people say about what you do? How is your reputation?

_____
_____
_____

Remember to answer these questions from the perspective of your ideal future.

5. Who / what kinds of people do you work with?

_____

_____

_____

6. What is your ultimate vision for the financial life you're headed toward (income, investments, savings, etc.)?

_____

_____

_____

_____

7. What sort of influence do you have on your community? What value do you bring to the world?

_____

_____

_____

_____

8. How do you feel about paying bills, taxes, or unforeseen expenses?

_____

_____

_____

9. How do you feel when you check your bank account?

_____

_____

_____

10. How do you spend your money in ways that make you feel you're having a positive impact?

_____

_____

_____

Relationship and Family

Projecting three years into the future of your happiest dreams, consider these details about how you want your love relationship and family life to be. Answer all the questions from this perspective – as if you have already attained this.

1. Describe your primary love relationship.

2. In this ideal relationship, what do you give, receive, create, and experience together? Consider all the realms of your relationship, including love, intimacy, friendship, support, play, etc.

3. How do you feel when you're talking with your partner? When you're expressing something that matters to you or makes you feel vulnerable?

4. How do you grow through being in this relationship?

Remember to answer these questions from the perspective of your ideal future.

5. In your ideal family life, how does it feel when everyone is home together?

_____
_____
_____
_____

6. What do you and your family members do together?

_____
_____
_____
_____

7. What are family conversations like? How does your family respond when you speak from your heart about something that is very important to you?

_____
_____
_____
_____

8. How does the family respond if someone has a problem?

_____
_____
_____
_____

9. What are holidays like together?

_____
_____
_____
_____

Community Connection

Projecting three years into the future of your most delighted dreams, consider these details about how you want your community to be. Answer all the questions from this perspective – as if you have already attained this.

1. What are your friendships like? What do you do together?

___
___
___
___
___

2. How prominently do your friends figure into your everyday life? How often to you get together?

___
___
___
___
___

3. How are your conversations? Are you able to share on all matters that concern you?

___
___
___
___
___

4. How do your friends respond when you're having a difficult time?

___
___
___
___
___

Remember to answer these questions from the perspective of your ideal future.

5. How do you and your friends support each other?

_____

_____

_____

6. What needs of yours are met by your friendships?

_____

_____

_____

7. Describe your community:

_____

_____

_____

_____

8. How do you engage with your community? In what way do you fit in?

_____

_____

_____

9. How are you nourished and/or supported by your community?

_____

_____

_____

10. What value do you bring to your community?

_____

_____

_____

Physical Wellness

Projecting three years into the future of your most healthy and vibrant dreams, consider these details about how you want your body, energy, and overall health to be. Answer all the questions from this perspective – as if you have already attained this.

1. Describe your beautiful body.

___

2. How do you feel in your body when you wake up in the morning?

___

3. How do you feel in your body at the end of a long day?

___

4. How is your relationship with exercise, and what do you do to keep your body in good shape?

___

5. How do you feed your body? What do you eat and *how* do you eat?

___

Remember to answer these questions from the perspective of your ideal future.

6. How is your energy?

___

7. How is your sleep?

___

8. How does it feel when you take a deep breath?

___

9. How are your strength and flexibility?

___

10. How do you feel about aging?

___

11. If you used to have any health problems, what has happened with these?

___

Creation, Exploration and Play

Projecting three years into the future of your most fun and fascinating dreams, consider these details about how you want to be engaging and expressing yourself creatively, intellectually, and playfully. Answer all the questions from this perspective – as if you have already attained this.

1. What percent of your life is reserved for playing, exploring, and creating?

_____

2. How much do you travel and to where?

_____
_____
_____

3. What forms of creative expression do you engage in (painting, drawing, sculpting, gardening, singing, playing an instrument, writing, acting, photography, dancing, building, sewing, etc.)?

_____
_____
_____
_____

4. How is your life affected by prioritizing creative expression, exploration, and play?

_____
_____
_____
_____

5. What forms of play and exploration do you engage in, and how often?

_____
_____
_____

Remember to answer these questions from the perspective of your ideal future.

6. Who else do you involve in your creative and playful endeavors and what role do they play?

7. Do you have a space just for doing your creative thing? What's it like?

8. What forums do you have for exploring the topics you're passionate about with others?

9. What fascinates you?

10. In what ways is your life beautiful and how do you live it in a beautiful way?

Psychological and Spiritual Health

Projecting three years into the future of your most lucid and uplifting dreams, consider these details about how you want to be thinking, feeling, and connecting. Answer all the questions from this perspective – as if you have already attained this.

1. What percentage of your waking life do you feel happy?

2. Describe your outlook on life & the quality of your thoughts:

3. What percentage of your communications come from a place of truth and love? And how does this affect you and others in your life?

4. How do you feel and respond during challenging times?

5. Do you trust yourself to manage whatever might happen?

6. What percentage of your life is spent in a peaceful state?

Remember to answer these questions from the perspective of your ideal future.

7. In what ways do you express love to others, the world, your higher power?

___

___

8. How is your life affected by your cultivating a more peaceful and loving experience?

___

___

9. How do you connect to your Higher Self, God, or The Universe? And what does it feel like?

___

___

___

10. How do you feel about the state of the world and your place in it?

___

___

___

11. How is your self-esteem?

___

___

12. How do you feel about the new day when you wake up in the morning?

___

___

13. How do you feel about dying?

___

___

___

CRAFT

Now, a message to you from your Highest Self:

Thank you for taking the time to let me express myself and make my deepest wishes known. I am absolutely ready to step into the reality you just wrote about. I know we can do it together! You might want to let me steer more often, though. I love you.

The material you came up with was not just a psychological exercise but a window to your true dreams. Use your answers to determine the qualities and behaviors you plan to cultivate from this day forward.

Now it's time to start crafting the tangible goals that align with your unique truth, gifts, and purpose. A mind map is a visual representation of ideas that makes it easy to organize concepts and connections. On the following pages, you are going to create maps of the goals you will achieve in the next year, in 3 years, in 10 years, and over your lifetime. Frame all goals in the positive – i.e., what you want to have, be, or do – not what you want to avoid or get rid of. Consider all the areas of your life we went through in the previous section: physical wellness; psychological and spiritual health; creation, exploration, and play; community connection; livelihood, career and influence; relationship and family. Here is an example:

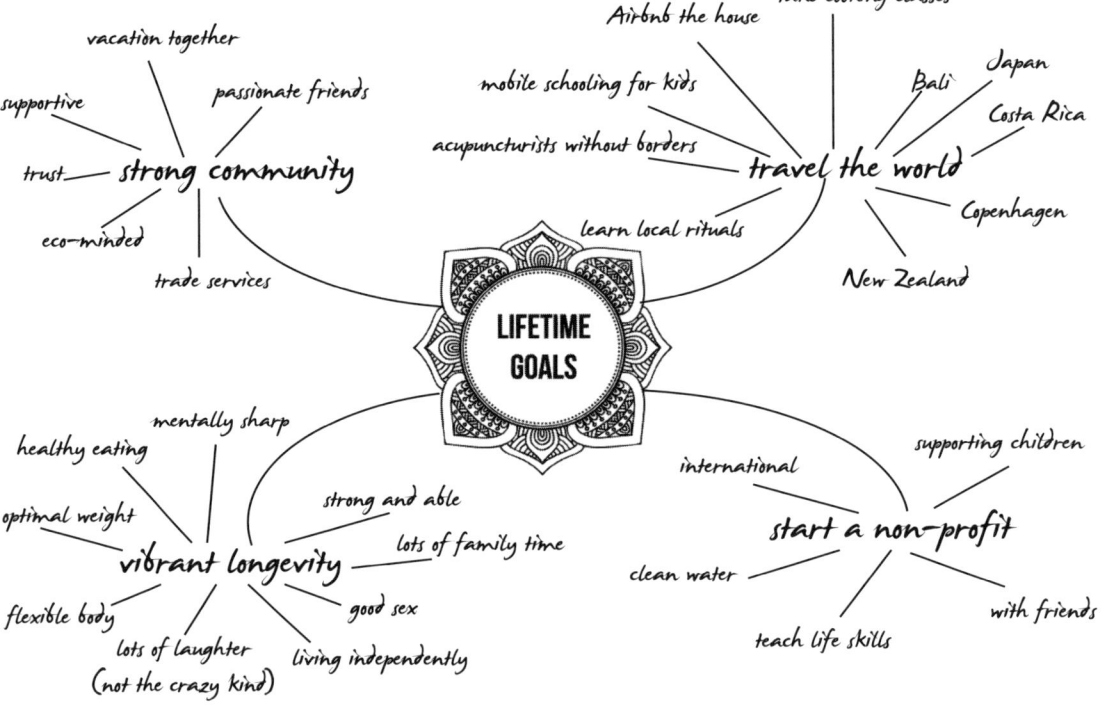

Break it Down

Simply recognizing how important these goals are to us doesn't necessarily ensure that we'll start knocking them out, meditating, eating better, and healing our relationship with our parents. We say this not to discourage you, but to explain that most people need more structure, more hand-holding, and more ritual in order to make this stuff stick.

That's why we'll immediately proceed to selecting goals, breaking these goals down into projects, breaking the projects down into actionable steps, getting these actions into your calendar, and forging rituals to stabilize your new paradigm.

Choose three goals from each mind map (life, 10 years, 3 years, and 1 year). Ask yourself, *why is **this** goal important to me?* When you've selected three, map each one with projects necessary to achieve this goal. Most of these projects will involve multiple actions, though some may be single actionable steps.

If you have a hard time considering how to reach a goal, start from the end result and work backwards. What would have to happen right before you reach your goal? And what would have to happen right before that? And right before that?

For each project, include your expected date of completion. These dates should be realistic, neither too loose nor too demanding. Set yourself up to succeed. Here's an example:

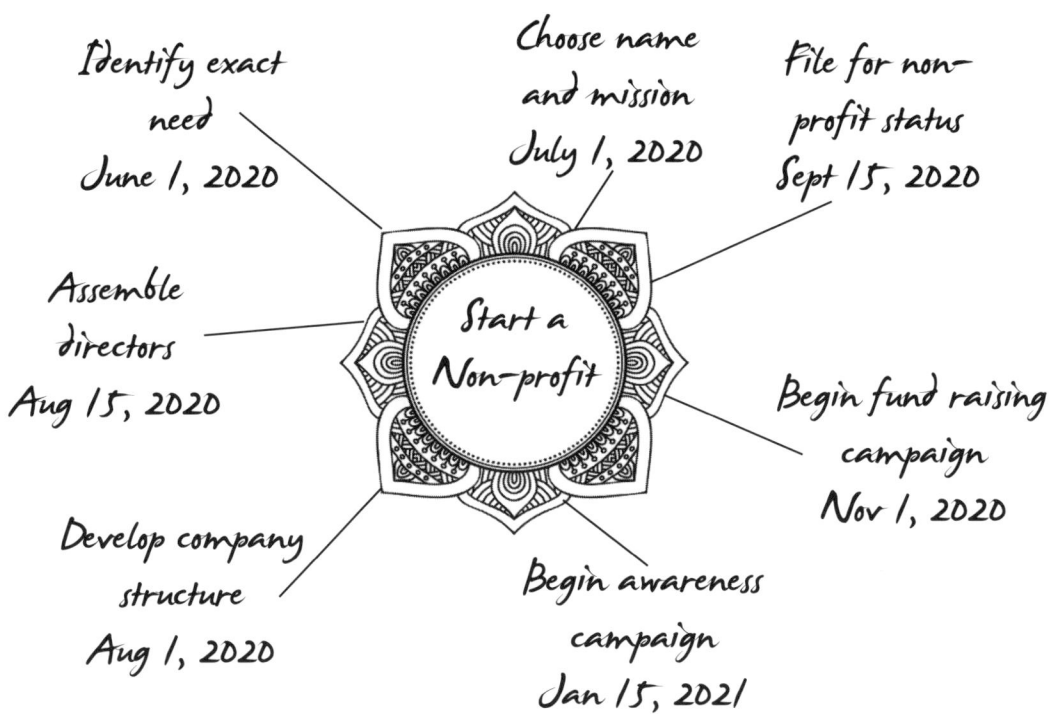

RITUALIZE

We've finally come to the Ritual part of Rituals for Living. This is where you get to make life more special for yourself. Many of us have an aversion to ritual because it seems to add extra time and energy to what we want to get done fast. If this is the case for you, we encourage you to ask yourself, *Where am I trying to get to so fast that I'm willing to sacrifice savoring the present?* It might also be worth considering whether the rituals around you, or the ones you've adopted from your family or community, aren't *yours*. If so, make up new ones that are meaningful and enjoyable for you. You will never regret taking the time for this.

Our top priority is to help you create a ritual around planning, but we encourage you to develop rituals around:

1. Any practice that you want to become more of a fixture in your life, such as exercise or cooking

2. Any everyday act that you want to enhance the specialness of, such as mealtimes or bathing

3. Any act that you want to transform into a grounding or tuning-in point in your life

As for planning, once a year simply isn't enough. In order to accomplish big things while maintaining a clean mental space, planning must become an integral part of your life. There's no reason to dread it – it can be enjoyable and can actually help you feel lighter. As soon as events change and the plan we've been working from needs modification, we feel a certain sense of unease until we check in and update the plan. It might be a very subtle feeling that's easy to ignore, but when we have major plans, the unease can feel quite strong. If something feels off, check in with your plan: Is something out of sync? Have you broken an agreement? Do you have a need that isn't being met? Revise the plan and/or your attitude. Clarity always feels good.

A ritual doesn't need to be ceremonious, but consider this: the more special you make your rituals, the more specialness there will be in your life. It's almost too simplistic to take it seriously, but it's true in so many areas of life, so we encourage you to let that sink in for a moment.

The most fundamental requirement of a ritual is that you're *deliberate* about it. This might mean that you tune in, take a single breath, and express to yourself what you intend to do. Then when you're done, you tune in, take a breath, and express that you have gratefully concluded the ritual. This could take literally ten seconds.

But adding additional elements that you're consistent about can make your rituals something you look forward to; it can make help cement your rituals more firmly into your life; and it can make it easier to quickly "drop in" to an efficient, lucid, or inspired state.

Consider the following elements for ideas. Think of them as ways to "bookend" your ritual, to set it apart from the everyday, and to lend greater potency to what you set out to do. These elements have set the stage for some of our most powerful planning and ideation sessions, our most efficient work, and our deepest meditations.

Fire: As a candle, a fireplace, an oil lamp, or the sun. Fire is a symbol of illumination, warmth, and connection.
Words: Set an intention, say a blessing or mantra, invoke a helper. Writing can make words even more "real."
Food or Drink: Consuming food/drink is special as it involves bringing something from the outside world into your body. Plus, it incorporates the senses of taste and smell, and may produce a biological response.
Beauty: Adorning and beautifying your space, your things, and your life is a way of elevating them beyond the mundane, and of demonstrating gratitude & reverence.
Sound: Trickling water, bells, chimes, chants, binaural beats, and favorite songs can all help tune our attention.
Garments: Putting on a special necklace, shawl, hat or superhero outfit may help you get into the right space.
Water: Water symbolizes purity, cleaning, and flow. Bathe, dip your hands in it, or splash some on your face.
Scents: Flowers, incense, and essential oils have long been used to uplift our consciousness and shift the space around us to designate a special purpose.
Gathering: Strength in numbers. Whether co-working or co-ritualizing, tuning in together can be stronger.
Location: The woods, the beach, or your altar in the bathroom. A consistent space can help focus your ritual.
Objects of Significance: A cup, a crystal, a lock of Bon Jovi's hair – these can help anchor you in your ritual.
Timing: Synchronizing a ritual with a particular season, the birthday of someone important, a historic event, a moon phase, time of day, the solstice, equinox, etc., may contribute to a sense of extra power and alignment.

Answer these questions to reveal factors that will be most natural for you to integrate into your rituals:

1. When and where do you feel your most inspired and focused?

_____

2. What clothing makes you feel most in your element? Sweats? Black tie? Kippa? Mala? Lucky socks?

_____

3. What's your favorite food or drink to consume while pondering your future & accessing your inner strength?

_____

4. Do you have any treasured objects that make you feel inspired or uplifted? Photo? Eagle feather?

_____

5. What helps you feel centered and grounded? Turning off your cell phone? Taking a bath? Running a mile?

_____

6. Are there any sounds or scents that help you relax or put you in a transcendent space?

_____

7. Which of the elements in the list above do you feel a natural attraction to?

_____
_____

What I Will Accomplish This Year

1. Get into your *ritual for planning* space. Do your thing (light a candle, take a breath, go to a peaceful spot, set an intention, etc.).

2. Flip back to the mind maps you created for the three goals you selected for the next one year, three years, ten years, and your lifetime. Mark any projects that will be *beginning or continuing* in coming year. Enter these projects in the table below and mark the appropriate number(s) for the quarter(s) in which the project will take place. (If you're starting this Dreambook at a time other than the beginning of a calendar year, first figure out which months each of your quarters comprises.)

Project	Quarter			
Example: *find a book agent*	①	●	③	④
	①	②	③	④
	①	②	③	④
	①	②	③	④
	①	②	③	④
	①	②	③	④
	①	②	③	④
	①	②	③	④
	①	②	③	④
	①	②	③	④
	①	②	③	④
	①	②	③	④
	①	②	③	④
	①	②	③	④

Project	Quarter			
	①	②	③	④
	①	②	③	④
	①	②	③	④
	①	②	③	④
	①	②	③	④
	①	②	③	④
	①	②	③	④
	①	②	③	④
	①	②	③	④
	①	②	③	④
	①	②	③	④
	①	②	③	④
	①	②	③	④
	①	②	③	④
	①	②	③	④
	①	②	③	④
	①	②	③	④
	①	②	③	④
	①	②	③	④

⟶ Theme of the Year ⟶

Set an intention for the coming year by giving it a theme. It's a good way to designate an overarching focus, and you may be surprised at how the experiences of the year fit the theme you choose. You can write your theme in the space below, and phrase it as such: "The Year of Learning to Love Myself" or "The Year of Forgiveness" or "The Year of Letting Go of the Struggle" or "The Year of Coming into My Power." Feel free to get artistic in how you write this. Go!

How to Work Your Plan

Much of this process will be spelled out in the following pages, but it's important to read this overview first.

1. Each quarter begins with a **Quarterly Breakdown**. This involves looking back at the goals you mapped previously, and writing down all the projects that will occur in the upcoming quarter.

2. For each project you'll then determine which of the three months of the quarter it will be getting worked on.

3. On the page for each month in the quarter, you'll write down each of the projects you've designated for that month, and you'll break each project down into *actionable tasks*.

4. Following each month's project breakdown, you'll see a two page **Monthly Calendar**. Write the name of the month at the left side. This calendar is blank so you can begin your year at any time (ideally the start of a quarter), so you'll need to write in the numbers for the days of the month. (You may occasionally have to the use one box for two days at the end of the month – such as May 2016. Drawing a diagonal line to divide the box in half may help.) You can record events and notes here, to be scheduled more precisely in the week view before each week begins.

5. After the month sections, you'll come to the **Weekly Calendar**. This will be used to plan each week (before the week begins!), and you'll refer back to this at least a couple times a day. Each week features:

   - The Focus Mandala. Here you can write a focus you choose for the week.
   - Top 3 Goals: Here you'll write three goals you intend to accomplish over the week (these are likely "small goals" compared to the ones you mapped, or might be the sub-projects of your larger goals).
   - Rituals for Living Challenge: A task for the week that's designed to nourish, expand, or heal your body and/or mind.
   - Tasks: Here you'll write the tasks that pertain to this week. These include:
     - Tasks from the project breakdown pages for your monthly plan
     - Leftover tasks to clean up from the previous week
     - All of your other life duties
   - When scheduling the coming week, you'll take everything from this task list and write it into the calendar with a beginning *and end* time – this will help keep the task from sprawling.
   - Rituals for Thriving – practices that are good for your body, mind, and soul – can be selected from the list on the page or you can come up with your own. These should be scheduled liberally into your week.
   - Intention for the Day: Here you can write an intention you have for each day. Keep it simple. It could even be a single word, like Breathe, Efficiency, Joy, Connect, Love, etc.
   - Morning Rituals and Activities: Here you will write any plans for before your work day begins. Often, this will include some Rituals for Thriving, such as exercise, journaling, meditation, cooking, etc.
   - Evening Rituals and Activities: Same thing but at the end of your day.
   - Gratitude: Here we encourage you to write one or more things you are grateful for each day. The more you express gratitude, the more aware you become of everything to be grateful for.
   - Dream, Expand, Record, Reflect: Use this space for notes, ideas, doodles, novel inventions, etc.
   - Please Note: In this version of the Dreambook+Planner, no dates are printed so that you can begin at any time. Write the month at the top of the page, and then fill in the date numbers in the empty boxes at the top of each day. Depending on how the weeks fall, you may have a month that spans two quarters.

6. DO IT WITH FRIENDS! Your chances of sticking with this will be better if you and one or more friends are all holding each other accountable.

7. Please visit our website – www.dreambook.vision – for more details about everything here, answers to your questions, exercises, and valuable resources.

Quarter One Breakdown

1. Get into your *ritual for planning* space. Do whatever you do to tune in (light a candle, take a breath, go to a peaceful spot, set an intention, etc.).

2. Look back at your What I Will Accomplish This Year list, and find all the projects that will be occurring in the coming quarter. Write each one in the table below and mark the appropriate month number(s) for the month(s) in which it will taking place. There is space at the top of the Month column to write abbreviations of the names of the months above ① ② and ③.

Project	Month		
	①	②	③
	①	②	③
	①	②	③
	①	②	③
	①	②	③
	①	②	③
	①	②	③
	①	②	③
	①	②	③
	①	②	③
	①	②	③
	①	②	③
	①	②	③
	①	②	③
	①	②	③
	①	②	③
	①	②	③
	①	②	③
	①	②	③
	①	②	③
	①	②	③
	①	②	③
	①	②	③
	①	②	③

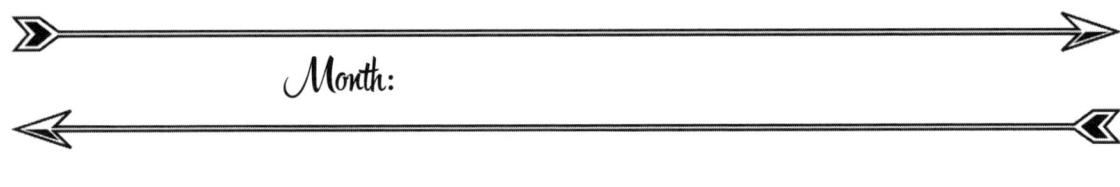

Month:

1. Get into your *ritual for planning* space.

2. Gather the projects from the Quarterly Breakdown that pertain to this month and write each one on a PROJECT line below.

3. Under the project name, enter all of the tasks that are involved in the project. Each of these tasks must be a single action step, so that it can be put into your calendar and when you see it, no analysis needs to occur – you know exactly what to do.

PROJECT

PROJECT

PROJECT

PROJECT

PROJECT

MONTH:

Monday	Tuesday	Wednesday

Notes:

Thursday	Friday	Saturday	Sunday

Month:

1. Get into your *ritual for planning* space.

2. Gather the projects from the Quarterly Breakdown that pertain to this month and write each one on a PROJECT line below.

3. Under the project name, enter all of the tasks that are involved in the project. Each of these tasks must be a single action step, so that it can be put into your calendar and when you see it, no analysis needs to occur – you know exactly what to do.

PROJECT

PROJECT

PROJECT

PROJECT

PROJECT

MONTH:

Monday	Tuesday	Wednesday

Notes:

Thursday	Friday	Saturday	Sunday

Month:

1. Get into your *ritual for planning* space.

2. Gather the projects from the Quarterly Breakdown that pertain to this month and write each one on a PROJECT line below.

3. Under the project name, enter all of the tasks that are involved in the project. Each of these tasks must be a single action step, so that it can be put into your calendar and when you see it, no analysis needs to occur – you know exactly what to do.

PROJECT

PROJECT

PROJECT

PROJECT

PROJECT

MONTH:

Monday	Tuesday	Wednesday

Notes:

Thursday	Friday	Saturday	Sunday

Rituals for Living Challenge
Sleep optimization. Get at least 7 hours every night. Wind down before bed with dim lights and quiet. No screens before or in bed. Keep your room dark and cool, no lights if you get up in the night. Sleep tight.

TOP 3 GOALS THIS WEEK

TASKS
- MONTHLY PLAN
- INCOMPLETE FROM LAST WEEK
- LIFE DUTIES
- ★ STAR THE MOST IMPORTANT TASKS ★

Final task: schedule next week

NOW: PUT THESE TASKS & RITUALS IN YOUR CALENDAR, GO FORTH AND CONQUER!

MONTH:

	MONDAY	TUESDAY	WEDNESDAY
	INTENTION:	INTENTION:	INTENTION:
	MORNING RITUALS AND ACTIVITIES	MORNING RITUALS AND ACTIVITIES	MORNING RITUALS AND ACTIVITIES
8:00			
8:30			
9:00			
9:30			
10:00			
10:30			
11:00			
11:30			
	WHAT SHALL I BE FOCUSED ON?	WHERE IS MY ATTENTION GOING?	WHAT PERSPECTIVE DO I CHOOSE?
12:00			
12:30			
1:00			
1:30			
2:00			
2:30			
3:00			
3:30			
4:00			
4:30			
5:00			
5:30			
6:00			
	EVENING RITUALS AND ACTIVITIES	EVENING RITUALS AND ACTIVITIES	EVENING RITUALS AND ACTIVITIES
	I AM GRATEFUL FOR:	I AM GRATEFUL FOR:	I AM GRATEFUL FOR:

RITUALS FOR THRIVING

- ○ EXERCISE
- ○ MEDITATE / BREATHE
- ○ JOURNAL
- ○ DANCE
- ○ GO ON A DATE
- ○ CONNECT WITH NATURE
- ○ VISUALIZE
- ○ FAMILY TIME
- ○ COOK / EAT A HEALTHY MEAL
- ○ ORGANIZE MY SPACE / LIFE
- ○ GET RID OF THINGS I DON'T LOVE
- ○ BE WITH FRIENDS
- ○ PLAY
- ○ LET GO / FORGIVE
- ○ SING / MAKE MUSIC
- ○ CREATE ART
- ○ READ FOR ENJOYMENT
- ○ CONNECT / PRAY
- ○ CALL SOMEONE / WRITE A LETTER
- ○ STRETCH / DO YOGA
- ○ MASSAGE / EXCHANGE TOUCH
- ○ SERVE MY COMMUNITY

THURSDAY	FRIDAY	SATURDAY
INTENTION:	INTENTION:	INTENTION:
MORNING RITUALS AND ACTIVITIES	MORNING RITUALS AND ACTIVITIES	MORNING RITUALS AND ACTIVITIES
8:00	8:00	
8:30	8:30	
9:00	9:00	
9:30	9:30	EVENING RITUALS AND ACTIVITIES
10:00	10:00	
10:30	10:30	
11:00	11:00	
11:30	11:30	I AM GRATEFUL FOR:
HOW AM I SPENDING MY ENERGY?	HOW DO I AFFECT MY WORLD?	
12:00	12:00	
12:30	12:30	
1:00	1:00	
1:30	1:30	
2:00	2:00	SUNDAY
2:30	2:30	INTENTION:
3:00	3:00	
3:30	3:30	
4:00	4:00	MORNING RITUALS AND ACTIVITIES
4:30	4:30	
5:00	5:00	
5:30	5:30	
6:00	6:00	
EVENING RITUALS AND ACTIVITIES	EVENING RITUALS AND ACTIVITIES	
		EVENING RITUALS AND ACTIVITIES
I AM GRATEFUL FOR:	I AM GRATEFUL FOR:	
		I AM GRATEFUL FOR:

DREAM, EXPAND, RECORD, REFLECT:

Rituals for Living Challenge

This week, buy as little in plastic containers as possible. Plastics can disrupt your endocrine system, and are extremely persistent in the environment. Most tap water is safe or can be easily made clean with a filter.

TOP 3 GOALS THIS WEEK

TASKS
- MONTHLY PLAN
- INCOMPLETE FROM LAST WEEK
- LIFE DUTIES
- ★ STAR THE MOST IMPORTANT TASKS ★

Final task: schedule next week

NOW: PUT THESE TASKS & RITUALS IN YOUR CALENDAR, GO FORTH AND CONQUER!

MONTH:

	MONDAY	TUESDAY	WEDNESDAY
	INTENTION:	INTENTION:	INTENTION:
	MORNING RITUALS AND ACTIVITIES	MORNING RITUALS AND ACTIVITIES	MORNING RITUALS AND ACTIVITIES
8:00			
8:30			
9:00			
9:30			
10:00			
10:30			
11:00			
11:30			
	WHAT SHALL I BE FOCUSED ON?	WHERE IS MY ATTENTION GOING?	WHAT PERSPECTIVE DO I CHOOSE?
12:00			
12:30			
1:00			
1:30			
2:00			
2:30			
3:00			
3:30			
4:00			
4:30			
5:00			
5:30			
6:00			
	EVENING RITUALS AND ACTIVITIES	EVENING RITUALS AND ACTIVITIES	EVENING RITUALS AND ACTIVITIES
	I AM GRATEFUL FOR:	I AM GRATEFUL FOR:	I AM GRATEFUL FOR:

RITUALS FOR THRIVING

- ○ EXERCISE
- ○ MEDITATE / BREATHE
- ○ JOURNAL
- ○ DANCE
- ○ GO ON A DATE
- ○ CONNECT WITH NATURE
- ○ VISUALIZE
- ○ FAMILY TIME
- ○ COOK / EAT A HEALTHY MEAL
- ○ ORGANIZE MY SPACE / LIFE
- ○ GET RID OF THINGS I DON'T LOVE
- ○ BE WITH FRIENDS
- ○ PLAY
- ○ LET GO / FORGIVE
- ○ SING / MAKE MUSIC
- ○ CREATE ART
- ○ READ FOR ENJOYMENT
- ○ CONNECT / PRAY
- ○ CALL SOMEONE / WRITE A LETTER
- ○ STRETCH / DO YOGA
- ○ MASSAGE / EXCHANGE TOUCH
- ○ SERVE MY COMMUNITY

THURSDAY	FRIDAY	SATURDAY
INTENTION:	INTENTION:	INTENTION:
MORNING RITUALS AND ACTIVITIES	MORNING RITUALS AND ACTIVITIES	MORNING RITUALS AND ACTIVITIES
8:00	8:00	
8:30	8:30	
9:00	9:00	
9:30	9:30	EVENING RITUALS AND ACTIVITIES
10:00	10:00	
10:30	10:30	
11:00	11:00	
11:30	11:30	I AM GRATEFUL FOR:
HOW AM I SPENDING MY ENERGY?	HOW DO I AFFECT MY WORLD?	
12:00	12:00	
12:30	12:30	
1:00	1:00	
1:30	1:30	
2:00	2:00	SUNDAY
2:30	2:30	INTENTION:
3:00	3:00	
3:30	3:30	
4:00	4:00	MORNING RITUALS AND ACTIVITIES
4:30	4:30	
5:00	5:00	
5:30	5:30	
6:00	6:00	
EVENING RITUALS AND ACTIVITIES	EVENING RITUALS AND ACTIVITIES	
		EVENING RITUALS AND ACTIVITIES
I AM GRATEFUL FOR:	I AM GRATEFUL FOR:	
		I AM GRATEFUL FOR:

DREAM, EXPAND, RECORD, REFLECT:

FOCUS

Rituals for Living Challenge
This week, create or refine your "sacred space." A place for you to tune in, center yourself, get grounded, meditate, and visualize. Make it appealing and conducive to peace.

TOP 3 GOALS THIS WEEK

TASKS
- MONTHLY PLAN
- INCOMPLETE FROM LAST WEEK
- LIFE DUTIES
- ★ STAR THE MOST IMPORTANT TASKS ★

Final task: schedule next week

NOW: PUT THESE TASKS & RITUALS IN YOUR CALENDAR, GO FORTH AND CONQUER!

MONTH:

	MONDAY	TUESDAY	WEDNESDAY
	INTENTION:	INTENTION:	INTENTION:
	MORNING RITUALS AND ACTIVITIES	MORNING RITUALS AND ACTIVITIES	MORNING RITUALS AND ACTIVITIES
8:00			
8:30			
9:00			
9:30			
10:00			
10:30			
11:00			
11:30			
	WHAT SHALL I BE FOCUSED ON?	WHERE IS MY ATTENTION GOING?	WHAT PERSPECTIVE DO I CHOOSE?
12:00			
12:30			
1:00			
1:30			
2:00			
2:30			
3:00			
3:30			
4:00			
4:30			
5:00			
5:30			
6:00			
	EVENING RITUALS AND ACTIVITIES	EVENING RITUALS AND ACTIVITIES	EVENING RITUALS AND ACTIVITIES
	I AM GRATEFUL FOR:	I AM GRATEFUL FOR:	I AM GRATEFUL FOR:

THURSDAY	FRIDAY	SATURDAY	RITUALS FOR THRIVING
INTENTION:	INTENTION:	INTENTION:	○ EXERCISE
			○ MEDITATE / BREATHE
MORNING RITUALS AND ACTIVITIES	MORNING RITUALS AND ACTIVITIES	MORNING RITUALS AND ACTIVITIES	○ JOURNAL
			○ DANCE
			○ GO ON A DATE
			○ CONNECT WITH NATURE
			○ VISUALIZE
			○ FAMILY TIME
			○ COOK / EAT A HEALTHY MEAL
			○ ORGANIZE MY SPACE / LIFE
8:00	8:00		○ GET RID OF THINGS I DON'T LOVE
8:30	8:30		○ BE WITH FRIENDS
9:00	9:00		○ PLAY
9:30	9:30	EVENING RITUALS AND ACTIVITIES	○ LET GO / FORGIVE
10:00	10:00		○ SING / MAKE MUSIC
10:30	10:30		○ CREATE ART
11:00	11:00		○ READ FOR ENJOYMENT
11:30	11:30	I AM GRATEFUL FOR:	○ CONNECT / PRAY
HOW AM I SPENDING MY ENERGY?	HOW DO I AFFECT MY WORLD?		○ CALL SOMEONE / WRITE A LETTER
12:00	12:00		○ STRETCH / DO YOGA
12:30	12:30		○ MASSAGE / EXCHANGE TOUCH
1:00	1:00		○ SERVE MY COMMUNITY
1:30	1:30		
2:00	2:00	SUNDAY	DREAM, EXPAND, RECORD, REFLECT:
2:30	2:30	INTENTION:	
3:00	3:00		
3:30	3:30		
4:00	4:00	MORNING RITUALS AND ACTIVITIES	
4:30	4:30		
5:00	5:00		
5:30	5:30		
6:00	6:00		
EVENING RITUALS AND ACTIVITIES	EVENING RITUALS AND ACTIVITIES		
		EVENING RITUALS AND ACTIVITIES	
I AM GRATEFUL FOR:	I AM GRATEFUL FOR:		
		I AM GRATEFUL FOR:	

FOCUS

Rituals for Living Challenge
This week, pay special attention to your posture. Tuck your chin a bit and lift the top of your head as if you were being suspended by a string. Let your chest and heart open. Carry yourself with purpose. Change your work station if necessary.

TOP 3 GOALS THIS WEEK

TASKS
- MONTHLY PLAN
- INCOMPLETE FROM LAST WEEK
- LIFE DUTIES
- ★ STAR THE MOST IMPORTANT TASKS ★

Final task: schedule next week

NOW: PUT THESE TASKS & RITUALS IN YOUR CALENDAR, GO FORTH AND CONQUER!

MONTH:

	MONDAY	TUESDAY	WEDNESDAY
	INTENTION:	INTENTION:	INTENTION:
	MORNING RITUALS AND ACTIVITIES	MORNING RITUALS AND ACTIVITIES	MORNING RITUALS AND ACTIVITIES
8:00			
8:30			
9:00			
9:30			
10:00			
10:30			
11:00			
11:30			
	WHAT SHALL I BE FOCUSED ON?	WHERE IS MY ATTENTION GOING?	WHAT PERSPECTIVE DO I CHOOSE?
12:00			
12:30			
1:00			
1:30			
2:00			
2:30			
3:00			
3:30			
4:00			
4:30			
5:00			
5:30			
6:00			
	EVENING RITUALS AND ACTIVITIES	EVENING RITUALS AND ACTIVITIES	EVENING RITUALS AND ACTIVITIES
	I AM GRATEFUL FOR:	I AM GRATEFUL FOR:	I AM GRATEFUL FOR:

RITUALS FOR THRIVING

- ○ EXERCISE
- ○ MEDITATE / BREATHE
- ○ JOURNAL
- ○ DANCE
- ○ GO ON A DATE
- ○ CONNECT WITH NATURE
- ○ VISUALIZE
- ○ FAMILY TIME
- ○ COOK / EAT A HEALTHY MEAL
- ○ ORGANIZE MY SPACE / LIFE
- ○ GET RID OF THINGS I DON'T LOVE
- ○ BE WITH FRIENDS
- ○ PLAY
- ○ LET GO / FORGIVE
- ○ SING / MAKE MUSIC
- ○ CREATE ART
- ○ READ FOR ENJOYMENT
- ○ CONNECT / PRAY
- ○ CALL SOMEONE / WRITE A LETTER
- ○ STRETCH / DO YOGA
- ○ MASSAGE / EXCHANGE TOUCH
- ○ SERVE MY COMMUNITY

THURSDAY	FRIDAY	SATURDAY
INTENTION:	INTENTION:	INTENTION:
MORNING RITUALS AND ACTIVITIES	MORNING RITUALS AND ACTIVITIES	MORNING RITUALS AND ACTIVITIES
8:00	8:00	
8:30	8:30	
9:00	9:00	
9:30	9:30	EVENING RITUALS AND ACTIVITIES
10:00	10:00	
10:30	10:30	
11:00	11:00	
11:30	11:30	I AM GRATEFUL FOR:
HOW AM I SPENDING MY ENERGY?	HOW DO I AFFECT MY WORLD?	
12:00	12:00	
12:30	12:30	
1:00	1:00	
1:30	1:30	
2:00	2:00	SUNDAY
2:30	2:30	INTENTION:
3:00	3:00	
3:30	3:30	
4:00	4:00	MORNING RITUALS AND ACTIVITIES
4:30	4:30	
5:00	5:00	
5:30	5:30	
6:00	6:00	
EVENING RITUALS AND ACTIVITIES	EVENING RITUALS AND ACTIVITIES	
		EVENING RITUALS AND ACTIVITIES
I AM GRATEFUL FOR:	I AM GRATEFUL FOR:	
		I AM GRATEFUL FOR:

DREAM, EXPAND, RECORD, REFLECT:

MONTH:

Rituals for Living Challenge

This week, hydrate. Divide the number of pounds you weigh in half and drink that many ounces of water each day. Metric: your weight in kg, divide by 30, drink that many liters of water per day.

TOP 3 GOALS THIS WEEK

TASKS
- MONTHLY PLAN
- INCOMPLETE FROM LAST WEEK
- LIFE DUTIES
- ★ STAR THE MOST IMPORTANT TASKS ★

Final task: schedule next week

NOW: PUT THESE TASKS & RITUALS IN YOUR CALENDAR, GO FORTH AND CONQUER!

	MONDAY	TUESDAY	WEDNESDAY
	INTENTION:	INTENTION:	INTENTION:
	MORNING RITUALS AND ACTIVITIES	MORNING RITUALS AND ACTIVITIES	MORNING RITUALS AND ACTIVITIES
8:00			
8:30			
9:00			
9:30			
10:00			
10:30			
11:00			
11:30			
	WHAT SHALL I BE FOCUSED ON?	WHERE IS MY ATTENTION GOING?	WHAT PERSPECTIVE DO I CHOOSE?
12:00			
12:30			
1:00			
1:30			
2:00			
2:30			
3:00			
3:30			
4:00			
4:30			
5:00			
5:30			
6:00			
	EVENING RITUALS AND ACTIVITIES	EVENING RITUALS AND ACTIVITIES	EVENING RITUALS AND ACTIVITIES
	I AM GRATEFUL FOR:	I AM GRATEFUL FOR:	I AM GRATEFUL FOR:

RITUALS FOR THRIVING

- ○ EXERCISE
- ○ MEDITATE / BREATHE
- ○ JOURNAL
- ○ DANCE
- ○ GO ON A DATE
- ○ CONNECT WITH NATURE
- ○ VISUALIZE
- ○ FAMILY TIME
- ○ COOK / EAT A HEALTHY MEAL
- ○ ORGANIZE MY SPACE / LIFE
- ○ GET RID OF THINGS I DON'T LOVE
- ○ BE WITH FRIENDS
- ○ PLAY
- ○ LET GO / FORGIVE
- ○ SING / MAKE MUSIC
- ○ CREATE ART
- ○ READ FOR ENJOYMENT
- ○ CONNECT / PRAY
- ○ CALL SOMEONE / WRITE A LETTER
- ○ STRETCH / DO YOGA
- ○ MASSAGE / EXCHANGE TOUCH
- ○ SERVE MY COMMUNITY

THURSDAY	FRIDAY	SATURDAY
INTENTION:	INTENTION:	INTENTION:
MORNING RITUALS AND ACTIVITIES	MORNING RITUALS AND ACTIVITIES	MORNING RITUALS AND ACTIVITIES
8:00	8:00	
8:30	8:30	
9:00	9:00	
9:30	9:30	EVENING RITUALS AND ACTIVITIES
10:00	10:00	
10:30	10:30	
11:00	11:00	
11:30	11:30	I AM GRATEFUL FOR:
HOW AM I SPENDING MY ENERGY?	HOW DO I AFFECT MY WORLD?	
12:00	12:00	
12:30	12:30	
1:00	1:00	
1:30	1:30	
2:00	2:00	SUNDAY
2:30	2:30	INTENTION:
3:00	3:00	
3:30	3:30	
4:00	4:00	MORNING RITUALS AND ACTIVITIES
4:30	4:30	
5:00	5:00	
5:30	5:30	
6:00	6:00	
EVENING RITUALS AND ACTIVITIES	EVENING RITUALS AND ACTIVITIES	
		EVENING RITUALS AND ACTIVITIES
I AM GRATEFUL FOR:	I AM GRATEFUL FOR:	
		I AM GRATEFUL FOR:

DREAM, EXPAND, RECORD, REFLECT:

Rituals for Living Challenge

This week, take a drama fast. Abstain from gossip, complaining, catastrophizing, sensationalizing. Tell your friends you sympathize but aren't going there. Avoid the news, or at least the tragic stuff.

TOP 3 GOALS THIS WEEK

TASKS
- MONTHLY PLAN
- INCOMPLETE FROM LAST WEEK
- LIFE DUTIES
- ★ STAR THE MOST IMPORTANT TASKS ★

Final task: schedule next week

NOW: PUT THESE TASKS & RITUALS IN YOUR CALENDAR, GO FORTH AND CONQUER!

MONTH:

	MONDAY	TUESDAY	WEDNESDAY
	INTENTION:	INTENTION:	INTENTION:
	MORNING RITUALS AND ACTIVITIES	MORNING RITUALS AND ACTIVITIES	MORNING RITUALS AND ACTIVITIES
8:00			
8:30			
9:00			
9:30			
10:00			
10:30			
11:00			
11:30			
	WHAT SHALL I BE FOCUSED ON?	WHERE IS MY ATTENTION GOING?	WHAT PERSPECTIVE DO I CHOOSE?
12:00			
12:30			
1:00			
1:30			
2:00			
2:30			
3:00			
3:30			
4:00			
4:30			
5:00			
5:30			
6:00			
	EVENING RITUALS AND ACTIVITIES	EVENING RITUALS AND ACTIVITIES	EVENING RITUALS AND ACTIVITIES
	I AM GRATEFUL FOR:	I AM GRATEFUL FOR:	I AM GRATEFUL FOR:

RITUALS FOR THRIVING

- ◯ EXERCISE
- ◯ MEDITATE / BREATHE
- ◯ JOURNAL
- ◯ DANCE
- ◯ GO ON A DATE
- ◯ CONNECT WITH NATURE
- ◯ VISUALIZE
- ◯ FAMILY TIME
- ◯ COOK / EAT A HEALTHY MEAL
- ◯ ORGANIZE MY SPACE / LIFE
- ◯ GET RID OF THINGS I DON'T LOVE
- ◯ BE WITH FRIENDS
- ◯ PLAY
- ◯ LET GO / FORGIVE
- ◯ SING / MAKE MUSIC
- ◯ CREATE ART
- ◯ READ FOR ENJOYMENT
- ◯ CONNECT / PRAY
- ◯ CALL SOMEONE / WRITE A LETTER
- ◯ STRETCH / DO YOGA
- ◯ MASSAGE / EXCHANGE TOUCH
- ◯ SERVE MY COMMUNITY

THURSDAY	FRIDAY	SATURDAY
INTENTION:	INTENTION:	INTENTION:
MORNING RITUALS AND ACTIVITIES	MORNING RITUALS AND ACTIVITIES	MORNING RITUALS AND ACTIVITIES
8:00	8:00	
8:30	8:30	
9:00	9:00	
9:30	9:30	EVENING RITUALS AND ACTIVITIES
10:00	10:00	
10:30	10:30	
11:00	11:00	
11:30	11:30	I AM GRATEFUL FOR:
HOW AM I SPENDING MY ENERGY?	HOW DO I AFFECT MY WORLD?	
12:00	12:00	
12:30	12:30	
1:00	1:00	
1:30	1:30	
2:00	2:00	SUNDAY
2:30	2:30	INTENTION:
3:00	3:00	
3:30	3:30	
4:00	4:00	MORNING RITUALS AND ACTIVITIES
4:30	4:30	
5:00	5:00	
5:30	5:30	
6:00	6:00	
EVENING RITUALS AND ACTIVITIES	EVENING RITUALS AND ACTIVITIES	
		EVENING RITUALS AND ACTIVITIES
I AM GRATEFUL FOR:	I AM GRATEFUL FOR:	
		I AM GRATEFUL FOR:

DREAM, EXPAND, RECORD, REFLECT:

Rituals for Living Challenge

This week, treat everyone you meet – bank tellers, friends, cashiers – as if they are an enlightened being. As if they have something profound to share with you. As if they have shown up in your life to teach or remind you of something.

TOP 3 GOALS THIS WEEK

TASKS
- MONTHLY PLAN
- INCOMPLETE FROM LAST WEEK
- LIFE DUTIES
- ★ STAR THE MOST IMPORTANT TASKS ★

Final task: schedule next week

NOW: PUT THESE TASKS & RITUALS IN YOUR CALENDAR, GO FORTH AND CONQUER!

MONTH:

	MONDAY	TUESDAY	WEDNESDAY
	INTENTION:	INTENTION:	INTENTION:
	MORNING RITUALS AND ACTIVITIES	MORNING RITUALS AND ACTIVITIES	MORNING RITUALS AND ACTIVITIES
8:00			
8:30			
9:00			
9:30			
10:00			
10:30			
11:00			
11:30			
	WHAT SHALL I BE FOCUSED ON?	WHERE IS MY ATTENTION GOING?	WHAT PERSPECTIVE DO I CHOOSE?
12:00			
12:30			
1:00			
1:30			
2:00			
2:30			
3:00			
3:30			
4:00			
4:30			
5:00			
5:30			
6:00			
	EVENING RITUALS AND ACTIVITIES	EVENING RITUALS AND ACTIVITIES	EVENING RITUALS AND ACTIVITIES
	I AM GRATEFUL FOR:	I AM GRATEFUL FOR:	I AM GRATEFUL FOR:

THURSDAY	FRIDAY	SATURDAY
INTENTION:	INTENTION:	INTENTION:
MORNING RITUALS AND ACTIVITIES	MORNING RITUALS AND ACTIVITIES	MORNING RITUALS AND ACTIVITIES
8:00	8:00	
8:30	8:30	
9:00	9:00	
9:30	9:30	EVENING RITUALS AND ACTIVITIES
10:00	10:00	
10:30	10:30	
11:00	11:00	
11:30	11:30	I AM GRATEFUL FOR:
HOW AM I SPENDING MY ENERGY?	HOW DO I AFFECT MY WORLD?	
12:00	12:00	
12:30	12:30	
1:00	1:00	
1:30	1:30	
2:00	2:00	SUNDAY
2:30	2:30	INTENTION:
3:00	3:00	
3:30	3:30	
4:00	4:00	MORNING RITUALS AND ACTIVITIES
4:30	4:30	
5:00	5:00	
5:30	5:30	
6:00	6:00	
EVENING RITUALS AND ACTIVITIES	EVENING RITUALS AND ACTIVITIES	
		EVENING RITUALS AND ACTIVITIES
I AM GRATEFUL FOR:	I AM GRATEFUL FOR:	
		I AM GRATEFUL FOR:

RITUALS FOR THRIVING

- ○ EXERCISE
- ○ MEDITATE / BREATHE
- ○ JOURNAL
- ○ DANCE
- ○ GO ON A DATE
- ○ CONNECT WITH NATURE
- ○ VISUALIZE
- ○ FAMILY TIME
- ○ COOK / EAT A HEALTHY MEAL
- ○ ORGANIZE MY SPACE / LIFE
- ○ GET RID OF THINGS I DON'T LOVE
- ○ BE WITH FRIENDS
- ○ PLAY
- ○ LET GO / FORGIVE
- ○ SING / MAKE MUSIC
- ○ CREATE ART
- ○ READ FOR ENJOYMENT
- ○ CONNECT / PRAY
- ○ CALL SOMEONE / WRITE A LETTER
- ○ STRETCH / DO YOGA
- ○ MASSAGE / EXCHANGE TOUCH
- ○ SERVE MY COMMUNITY

DREAM, EXPAND, RECORD, REFLECT:

Rituals for Living Challenge

Green smoothie 5 times this week: BIG handful of spinach, handful of whole fruit (banana, mango, berries, etc.), dash of lemon, slice of ginger, add water to make 1 quart/liter. (Drop of honey ok.) Blend until smooth. Drink slowly.

TOP 3 GOALS THIS WEEK

TASKS
- MONTHLY PLAN
- INCOMPLETE FROM LAST WEEK
- LIFE DUTIES
- ★ STAR THE MOST IMPORTANT TASKS ★

Final task: schedule next week

NOW: PUT THESE TASKS & RITUALS IN YOUR CALENDAR, GO FORTH AND CONQUER!

MONTH:

	MONDAY	TUESDAY	WEDNESDAY
	INTENTION:	INTENTION:	INTENTION:
	MORNING RITUALS AND ACTIVITIES	MORNING RITUALS AND ACTIVITIES	MORNING RITUALS AND ACTIVITIES
8:00			
8:30			
9:00			
9:30			
10:00			
10:30			
11:00			
11:30			
	WHAT SHALL I BE FOCUSED ON?	WHERE IS MY ATTENTION GOING?	WHAT PERSPECTIVE DO I CHOOSE?
12:00			
12:30			
1:00			
1:30			
2:00			
2:30			
3:00			
3:30			
4:00			
4:30			
5:00			
5:30			
6:00			
	EVENING RITUALS AND ACTIVITIES	EVENING RITUALS AND ACTIVITIES	EVENING RITUALS AND ACTIVITIES
	I AM GRATEFUL FOR:	I AM GRATEFUL FOR:	I AM GRATEFUL FOR:

THURSDAY	FRIDAY	SATURDAY
INTENTION:	INTENTION:	INTENTION:
MORNING RITUALS AND ACTIVITIES	MORNING RITUALS AND ACTIVITIES	MORNING RITUALS AND ACTIVITIES
8:00	8:00	
8:30	8:30	
9:00	9:00	
9:30	9:30	EVENING RITUALS AND ACTIVITIES
10:00	10:00	
10:30	10:30	
11:00	11:00	
11:30	11:30	I AM GRATEFUL FOR:
HOW AM I SPENDING MY ENERGY?	HOW DO I AFFECT MY WORLD?	
12:00	12:00	
12:30	12:30	
1:00	1:00	
1:30	1:30	
2:00	2:00	SUNDAY
2:30	2:30	INTENTION:
3:00	3:00	
3:30	3:30	
4:00	4:00	MORNING RITUALS AND ACTIVITIES
4:30	4:30	
5:00	5:00	
5:30	5:30	
6:00	6:00	
EVENING RITUALS AND ACTIVITIES	EVENING RITUALS AND ACTIVITIES	
		EVENING RITUALS AND ACTIVITIES
I AM GRATEFUL FOR:	I AM GRATEFUL FOR:	
		I AM GRATEFUL FOR:

RITUALS FOR THRIVING

- ○ EXERCISE
- ○ MEDITATE / BREATHE
- ○ JOURNAL
- ○ DANCE
- ○ GO ON A DATE
- ○ CONNECT WITH NATURE
- ○ VISUALIZE
- ○ FAMILY TIME
- ○ COOK / EAT A HEALTHY MEAL
- ○ ORGANIZE MY SPACE / LIFE
- ○ GET RID OF THINGS I DON'T LOVE
- ○ BE WITH FRIENDS
- ○ PLAY
- ○ LET GO / FORGIVE
- ○ SING / MAKE MUSIC
- ○ CREATE ART
- ○ READ FOR ENJOYMENT
- ○ CONNECT / PRAY
- ○ CALL SOMEONE / WRITE A LETTER
- ○ STRETCH / DO YOGA
- ○ MASSAGE / EXCHANGE TOUCH
- ○ SERVE MY COMMUNITY

DREAM, EXPAND, RECORD, REFLECT:

Rituals for Living Challenge

This week, reach out: Connect with three people you've been out of touch with. Tell them you're glad to have them in your life.

TOP 3 GOALS THIS WEEK

TASKS
- MONTHLY PLAN
- INCOMPLETE FROM LAST WEEK
- LIFE DUTIES
- ★ STAR THE MOST IMPORTANT TASKS ★

Final task: schedule next week

NOW: PUT THESE TASKS & RITUALS IN YOUR CALENDAR, GO FORTH AND CONQUER!

MONTH:

	MONDAY	TUESDAY	WEDNESDAY
	INTENTION:	INTENTION:	INTENTION:
	MORNING RITUALS AND ACTIVITIES	MORNING RITUALS AND ACTIVITIES	MORNING RITUALS AND ACTIVITIES
8:00			
8:30			
9:00			
9:30			
10:00			
10:30			
11:00			
11:30			
	WHAT SHALL I BE FOCUSED ON?	WHERE IS MY ATTENTION GOING?	WHAT PERSPECTIVE DO I CHOOSE?
12:00			
12:30			
1:00			
1:30			
2:00			
2:30			
3:00			
3:30			
4:00			
4:30			
5:00			
5:30			
6:00			
	EVENING RITUALS AND ACTIVITIES	EVENING RITUALS AND ACTIVITIES	EVENING RITUALS AND ACTIVITIES
	I AM GRATEFUL FOR:	I AM GRATEFUL FOR:	I AM GRATEFUL FOR:

THURSDAY	FRIDAY	SATURDAY
INTENTION:	INTENTION:	INTENTION:
MORNING RITUALS AND ACTIVITIES	MORNING RITUALS AND ACTIVITIES	MORNING RITUALS AND ACTIVITIES
8:00	8:00	
8:30	8:30	
9:00	9:00	
9:30	9:30	EVENING RITUALS AND ACTIVITIES
10:00	10:00	
10:30	10:30	
11:00	11:00	
11:30	11:30	I AM GRATEFUL FOR:
HOW AM I SPENDING MY ENERGY?	HOW DO I AFFECT MY WORLD?	
12:00	12:00	
12:30	12:30	
1:00	1:00	
1:30	1:30	
2:00	2:00	SUNDAY
2:30	2:30	INTENTION:
3:00	3:00	
3:30	3:30	
4:00	4:00	MORNING RITUALS AND ACTIVITIES
4:30	4:30	
5:00	5:00	
5:30	5:30	
6:00	6:00	
EVENING RITUALS AND ACTIVITIES	EVENING RITUALS AND ACTIVITIES	
		EVENING RITUALS AND ACTIVITIES
I AM GRATEFUL FOR:	I AM GRATEFUL FOR:	
		I AM GRATEFUL FOR:

RITUALS FOR THRIVING

- ○ EXERCISE
- ○ MEDITATE / BREATHE
- ○ JOURNAL
- ○ DANCE
- ○ GO ON A DATE
- ○ CONNECT WITH NATURE
- ○ VISUALIZE
- ○ FAMILY TIME
- ○ COOK / EAT A HEALTHY MEAL
- ○ ORGANIZE MY SPACE / LIFE
- ○ GET RID OF THINGS I DON'T LOVE
- ○ BE WITH FRIENDS
- ○ PLAY
- ○ LET GO / FORGIVE
- ○ SING / MAKE MUSIC
- ○ CREATE ART
- ○ READ FOR ENJOYMENT
- ○ CONNECT / PRAY
- ○ CALL SOMEONE / WRITE A LETTER
- ○ STRETCH / DO YOGA
- ○ MASSAGE / EXCHANGE TOUCH
- ○ SERVE MY COMMUNITY

DREAM, EXPAND, RECORD, REFLECT:

FOCUS

....
Rituals for Living Challenge
This week, serve. Find a way to do something in service to your community. Examples: volunteer at a shelter, shovel an elderly neighbor's driveway, repair a public bench, pick up litter on your morning walk. Get creative.
....

TOP 3 GOALS THIS WEEK

TASKS
- MONTHLY PLAN
- INCOMPLETE FROM LAST WEEK
- LIFE DUTIES
- ★ STAR THE MOST IMPORTANT TASKS ★

Final task: schedule next week
NOW: PUT THESE TASKS & RITUALS IN YOUR CALENDAR, GO FORTH AND CONQUER!

MONTH:

	MONDAY	TUESDAY	WEDNESDAY
	INTENTION:	INTENTION:	INTENTION:
	MORNING RITUALS AND ACTIVITIES	MORNING RITUALS AND ACTIVITIES	MORNING RITUALS AND ACTIVITIES
8:00			
8:30			
9:00			
9:30			
10:00			
10:30			
11:00			
11:30			
	WHAT SHALL I BE FOCUSED ON?	WHERE IS MY ATTENTION GOING?	WHAT PERSPECTIVE DO I CHOOSE?
12:00			
12:30			
1:00			
1:30			
2:00			
2:30			
3:00			
3:30			
4:00			
4:30			
5:00			
5:30			
6:00			
	EVENING RITUALS AND ACTIVITIES	EVENING RITUALS AND ACTIVITIES	EVENING RITUALS AND ACTIVITIES
	I AM GRATEFUL FOR:	I AM GRATEFUL FOR:	I AM GRATEFUL FOR:

RITUALS FOR THRIVING

- ○ EXERCISE
- ○ MEDITATE / BREATHE
- ○ JOURNAL
- ○ DANCE
- ○ GO ON A DATE
- ○ CONNECT WITH NATURE
- ○ VISUALIZE
- ○ FAMILY TIME
- ○ COOK / EAT A HEALTHY MEAL
- ○ ORGANIZE MY SPACE / LIFE
- ○ GET RID OF THINGS I DON'T LOVE
- ○ BE WITH FRIENDS
- ○ PLAY
- ○ LET GO / FORGIVE
- ○ SING / MAKE MUSIC
- ○ CREATE ART
- ○ READ FOR ENJOYMENT
- ○ CONNECT / PRAY
- ○ CALL SOMEONE / WRITE A LETTER
- ○ STRETCH / DO YOGA
- ○ MASSAGE / EXCHANGE TOUCH
- ○ SERVE MY COMMUNITY

THURSDAY	FRIDAY	SATURDAY
INTENTION:	INTENTION:	INTENTION:
MORNING RITUALS AND ACTIVITIES	MORNING RITUALS AND ACTIVITIES	MORNING RITUALS AND ACTIVITIES
8:00	8:00	
8:30	8:30	
9:00	9:00	
9:30	9:30	EVENING RITUALS AND ACTIVITIES
10:00	10:00	
10:30	10:30	
11:00	11:00	
11:30	11:30	I AM GRATEFUL FOR:
HOW AM I SPENDING MY ENERGY?	HOW DO I AFFECT MY WORLD?	
12:00	12:00	
12:30	12:30	
1:00	1:00	
1:30	1:30	
2:00	2:00	SUNDAY
2:30	2:30	INTENTION:
3:00	3:00	
3:30	3:30	
4:00	4:00	MORNING RITUALS AND ACTIVITIES
4:30	4:30	
5:00	5:00	
5:30	5:30	
6:00	6:00	
EVENING RITUALS AND ACTIVITIES	EVENING RITUALS AND ACTIVITIES	
		EVENING RITUALS AND ACTIVITIES
I AM GRATEFUL FOR:	I AM GRATEFUL FOR:	
		I AM GRATEFUL FOR:

DREAM, EXPAND, RECORD, REFLECT:

FOCUS

Rituals for Living Challenge
This week: breathe.
Once each day, close your eyes and take ten full breaths, inhaling deeply into your belly. Let your exhale be longer than your inhale.

TOP 3 GOALS THIS WEEK

TASKS
- MONTHLY PLAN
- INCOMPLETE FROM LAST WEEK
- LIFE DUTIES
- ★ STAR THE MOST IMPORTANT TASKS ★

Final task: schedule next week
NOW: PUT THESE TASKS & RITUALS IN YOUR CALENDAR, GO FORTH AND CONQUER!

MONTH:

	MONDAY	TUESDAY	WEDNESDAY
	INTENTION:	INTENTION:	INTENTION:
	MORNING RITUALS AND ACTIVITIES	MORNING RITUALS AND ACTIVITIES	MORNING RITUALS AND ACTIVITIES
8:00			
8:30			
9:00			
9:30			
10:00			
10:30			
11:00			
11:30			
	WHAT SHALL I BE FOCUSED ON?	WHERE IS MY ATTENTION GOING?	WHAT PERSPECTIVE DO I CHOOSE?
12:00			
12:30			
1:00			
1:30			
2:00			
2:30			
3:00			
3:30			
4:00			
4:30			
5:00			
5:30			
6:00			
	EVENING RITUALS AND ACTIVITIES	EVENING RITUALS AND ACTIVITIES	EVENING RITUALS AND ACTIVITIES
	I AM GRATEFUL FOR:	I AM GRATEFUL FOR:	I AM GRATEFUL FOR:

RITUALS FOR THRIVING

- ○ EXERCISE
- ○ MEDITATE / BREATHE
- ○ JOURNAL
- ○ DANCE
- ○ GO ON A DATE
- ○ CONNECT WITH NATURE
- ○ VISUALIZE
- ○ FAMILY TIME
- ○ COOK / EAT A HEALTHY MEAL
- ○ ORGANIZE MY SPACE / LIFE
- ○ GET RID OF THINGS I DON'T LOVE
- ○ BE WITH FRIENDS
- ○ PLAY
- ○ LET GO / FORGIVE
- ○ SING / MAKE MUSIC
- ○ CREATE ART
- ○ READ FOR ENJOYMENT
- ○ CONNECT / PRAY
- ○ CALL SOMEONE / WRITE A LETTER
- ○ STRETCH / DO YOGA
- ○ MASSAGE / EXCHANGE TOUCH
- ○ SERVE MY COMMUNITY

THURSDAY	FRIDAY	SATURDAY
INTENTION:	INTENTION:	INTENTION:
MORNING RITUALS AND ACTIVITIES	MORNING RITUALS AND ACTIVITIES	MORNING RITUALS AND ACTIVITIES
8:00	8:00	
8:30	8:30	
9:00	9:00	
9:30	9:30	EVENING RITUALS AND ACTIVITIES
10:00	10:00	
10:30	10:30	
11:00	11:00	
11:30	11:30	I AM GRATEFUL FOR:
HOW AM I SPENDING MY ENERGY?	HOW DO I AFFECT MY WORLD?	
12:00	12:00	
12:30	12:30	
1:00	1:00	
1:30	1:30	
2:00	2:00	SUNDAY
2:30	2:30	INTENTION:
3:00	3:00	
3:30	3:30	
4:00	4:00	MORNING RITUALS AND ACTIVITIES
4:30	4:30	
5:00	5:00	
5:30	5:30	
6:00	6:00	
EVENING RITUALS AND ACTIVITIES	EVENING RITUALS AND ACTIVITIES	
		EVENING RITUALS AND ACTIVITIES
I AM GRATEFUL FOR:	I AM GRATEFUL FOR:	
		I AM GRATEFUL FOR:

DREAM, EXPAND, RECORD, REFLECT:

Rituals for Living Challenge

This week, feed your body good things. Each day replace one not-so-healthy thing with a healthy thing. If you already do this, each day try a new fruit, vegetable, or spice. If there aren't any you haven't tried, try a new recipe.

TOP 3 GOALS THIS WEEK

TASKS
- MONTHLY PLAN
- INCOMPLETE FROM LAST WEEK
- LIFE DUTIES
- ★ STAR THE MOST IMPORTANT TASKS ★

Final task: schedule next week

NOW: PUT THESE TASKS & RITUALS IN YOUR CALENDAR, GO FORTH AND CONQUER!

MONTH:

	MONDAY	TUESDAY	WEDNESDAY
	INTENTION:	INTENTION:	INTENTION:
	MORNING RITUALS AND ACTIVITIES	MORNING RITUALS AND ACTIVITIES	MORNING RITUALS AND ACTIVITIES
8:00			
8:30			
9:00			
9:30			
10:00			
10:30			
11:00			
11:30			
	WHAT SHALL I BE FOCUSED ON?	WHERE IS MY ATTENTION GOING?	WHAT PERSPECTIVE DO I CHOOSE?
12:00			
12:30			
1:00			
1:30			
2:00			
2:30			
3:00			
3:30			
4:00			
4:30			
5:00			
5:30			
6:00			
	EVENING RITUALS AND ACTIVITIES	EVENING RITUALS AND ACTIVITIES	EVENING RITUALS AND ACTIVITIES
	I AM GRATEFUL FOR:	I AM GRATEFUL FOR:	I AM GRATEFUL FOR:

RITUALS FOR THRIVING

- ○ EXERCISE
- ○ MEDITATE / BREATHE
- ○ JOURNAL
- ○ DANCE
- ○ GO ON A DATE
- ○ CONNECT WITH NATURE
- ○ VISUALIZE
- ○ FAMILY TIME
- ○ COOK / EAT A HEALTHY MEAL
- ○ ORGANIZE MY SPACE / LIFE
- ○ GET RID OF THINGS I DON'T LOVE
- ○ BE WITH FRIENDS
- ○ PLAY
- ○ LET GO / FORGIVE
- ○ SING / MAKE MUSIC
- ○ CREATE ART
- ○ READ FOR ENJOYMENT
- ○ CONNECT / PRAY
- ○ CALL SOMEONE / WRITE A LETTER
- ○ STRETCH / DO YOGA
- ○ MASSAGE / EXCHANGE TOUCH
- ○ SERVE MY COMMUNITY

THURSDAY	FRIDAY	SATURDAY
INTENTION:	INTENTION:	INTENTION:
MORNING RITUALS AND ACTIVITIES	MORNING RITUALS AND ACTIVITIES	MORNING RITUALS AND ACTIVITIES
8:00	8:00	
8:30	8:30	
9:00	9:00	
9:30	9:30	EVENING RITUALS AND ACTIVITIES
10:00	10:00	
10:30	10:30	
11:00	11:00	
11:30	11:30	I AM GRATEFUL FOR:
HOW AM I SPENDING MY ENERGY?	HOW DO I AFFECT MY WORLD?	
12:00	12:00	
12:30	12:30	
1:00	1:00	
1:30	1:30	
2:00	2:00	SUNDAY
2:30	2:30	INTENTION:
3:00	3:00	
3:30	3:30	
4:00	4:00	MORNING RITUALS AND ACTIVITIES
4:30	4:30	
5:00	5:00	
5:30	5:30	
6:00	6:00	
EVENING RITUALS AND ACTIVITIES	EVENING RITUALS AND ACTIVITIES	
		EVENING RITUALS AND ACTIVITIES
I AM GRATEFUL FOR:	I AM GRATEFUL FOR:	
		I AM GRATEFUL FOR:

DREAM, EXPAND, RECORD, REFLECT:

Rituals for Living Challenge

This week, make up a song or poem. If this is not something you'd normally do, think of it as an exercise that challenges the wiring of your brain and stretches your comfort zone. If you are brave enough, share it with someone.

TOP 3 GOALS THIS WEEK

TASKS
- MONTHLY PLAN
- INCOMPLETE FROM LAST WEEK
- LIFE DUTIES
- ★ STAR THE MOST IMPORTANT TASKS ★

Final task: schedule next week

NOW: PUT THESE TASKS & RITUALS IN YOUR CALENDAR, GO FORTH AND CONQUER!

MONTH:

	MONDAY	TUESDAY	WEDNESDAY
	INTENTION:	**INTENTION:**	**INTENTION:**
	MORNING RITUALS AND ACTIVITIES	**MORNING RITUALS AND ACTIVITIES**	**MORNING RITUALS AND ACTIVITIES**
8:00			
8:30			
9:00			
9:30			
10:00			
10:30			
11:00			
11:30			
	WHAT SHALL I BE FOCUSED ON?	WHERE IS MY ATTENTION GOING?	WHAT PERSPECTIVE DO I CHOOSE?
12:00			
12:30			
1:00			
1:30			
2:00			
2:30			
3:00			
3:30			
4:00			
4:30			
5:00			
5:30			
6:00			
	EVENING RITUALS AND ACTIVITIES	**EVENING RITUALS AND ACTIVITIES**	**EVENING RITUALS AND ACTIVITIES**
	I AM GRATEFUL FOR:	**I AM GRATEFUL FOR:**	**I AM GRATEFUL FOR:**

RITUALS FOR THRIVING

- ○ EXERCISE
- ○ MEDITATE / BREATHE
- ○ JOURNAL
- ○ DANCE
- ○ GO ON A DATE
- ○ CONNECT WITH NATURE
- ○ VISUALIZE
- ○ FAMILY TIME
- ○ COOK / EAT A HEALTHY MEAL
- ○ ORGANIZE MY SPACE / LIFE
- ○ GET RID OF THINGS I DON'T LOVE
- ○ BE WITH FRIENDS
- ○ PLAY
- ○ LET GO / FORGIVE
- ○ SING / MAKE MUSIC
- ○ CREATE ART
- ○ READ FOR ENJOYMENT
- ○ CONNECT / PRAY
- ○ CALL SOMEONE / WRITE A LETTER
- ○ STRETCH / DO YOGA
- ○ MASSAGE / EXCHANGE TOUCH
- ○ SERVE MY COMMUNITY

THURSDAY	FRIDAY	SATURDAY
INTENTION:	INTENTION:	INTENTION:
MORNING RITUALS AND ACTIVITIES	MORNING RITUALS AND ACTIVITIES	MORNING RITUALS AND ACTIVITIES
8:00	8:00	
8:30	8:30	
9:00	9:00	
9:30	9:30	EVENING RITUALS AND ACTIVITIES
10:00	10:00	
10:30	10:30	
11:00	11:00	
11:30	11:30	I AM GRATEFUL FOR:
HOW AM I SPENDING MY ENERGY?	HOW DO I AFFECT MY WORLD?	
12:00	12:00	
12:30	12:30	
1:00	1:00	
1:30	1:30	
2:00	2:00	SUNDAY
2:30	2:30	INTENTION:
3:00	3:00	
3:30	3:30	
4:00	4:00	MORNING RITUALS AND ACTIVITIES
4:30	4:30	
5:00	5:00	
5:30	5:30	
6:00	6:00	
EVENING RITUALS AND ACTIVITIES	EVENING RITUALS AND ACTIVITIES	
		EVENING RITUALS AND ACTIVITIES
I AM GRATEFUL FOR:	I AM GRATEFUL FOR:	
		I AM GRATEFUL FOR:

DREAM, EXPAND, RECORD, REFLECT:

It's time to reflect on the past quarter and decide what you want to refine as you move forward.

1. What was your biggest time and/or energy waster in the past quarter?

_____

_____

2. Which activities and rituals yielded the biggest "return" for you (either tangible or intangible) in the past quarter?

_____

_____

3. Is there anything you've been procrastinating over the past quarter?

_____

_____

4. Which of the items from the Rituals for Thriving list did you never do but would like to?

_____

_____

5. If anything happened in the last quarter that you would like to *reframe* (i.e., change the story you tell yourself and others about it, so as to hold it in a more positive light), please write how you intend to reframe it.

_____

_____

_____

6. What has been infringing on your happiness, health, or productivity in the past quarter that you intend to let go of in the coming quarter?

_____

_____

_____

NOW, use these answers to shape your focus and refine your
thoughts and behaviors in the coming quarter!

Quarter Two Breakdown

1. Get into your *ritual for planning* space. Do whatever you do to tune in (light a candle, take a breath, go to a peaceful spot, set an intention, etc.).

2. Look back at your What I Will Accomplish This Year list, and find all the projects that will be occurring in the coming quarter. Write each one in the table below and mark the appropriate month number(s) for the month(s) in which it will taking place. There is space at the top of the Month column to write abbreviations of the names of the months above ① ② and ③.

Project	Month		
	①	②	③
	①	②	③
	①	②	③
	①	②	③
	①	②	③
	①	②	③
	①	②	③
	①	②	③
	①	②	③
	①	②	③
	①	②	③
	①	②	③
	①	②	③
	①	②	③
	①	②	③
	①	②	③
	①	②	③
	①	②	③
	①	②	③
	①	②	③
	①	②	③
	①	②	③
	①	②	③

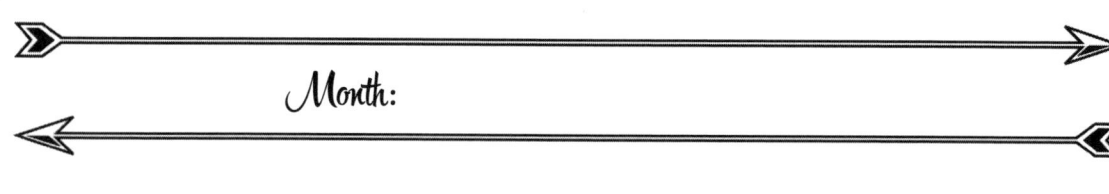

Month:

1. Get into your *ritual for planning* space.

2. Gather the projects from the Quarterly Breakdown that pertain to this month and write each one on a PROJECT line below.

3. Under the project name, enter all of the tasks that are involved in the project. Each of these tasks must be a single action step, so that it can be put into your calendar and when you see it, no analysis needs to occur – you know exactly what to do.

PROJECT

PROJECT

PROJECT

PROJECT

PROJECT

MONTH:

Monday	Tuesday	Wednesday

Notes:

Thursday	Friday	Saturday	Sunday

Month:

1. Get into your *ritual for planning* space.

2. Gather the projects from the Quarterly Breakdown that pertain to this month and write each one on a PROJECT line below.

3. Under the project name, enter all of the tasks that are involved in the project. Each of these tasks must be a single action step, so that it can be put into your calendar and when you see it, no analysis needs to occur – you know exactly what to do.

_____
PROJECT

_____ _____
_____ _____
_____ _____
_____ _____
_____ _____
_____ _____
_____ _____
_____ _____

_____
PROJECT

_____ _____
_____ _____
_____ _____
_____ _____
_____ _____
_____ _____
_____ _____
_____ _____

PROJECT

PROJECT

PROJECT

MONTH:

Monday	Tuesday	Wednesday

Notes:

Thursday	Friday	Saturday	Sunday

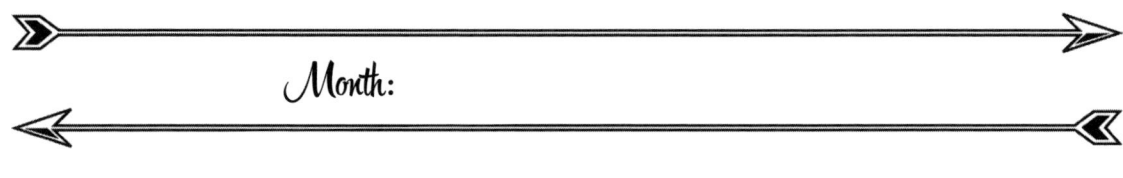

Month:

1. Get into your *ritual for planning* space.

2. Gather the projects from the Quarterly Breakdown that pertain to this month and write each one on a PROJECT line below.

3. Under the project name, enter all of the tasks that are involved in the project. Each of these tasks must be a single action step, so that it can be put into your calendar and when you see it, no analysis needs to occur – you know exactly what to do.

PROJECT
_____ _____
_____ _____
_____ _____
_____ _____
_____ _____
_____ _____
_____ _____

PROJECT
_____ _____
_____ _____
_____ _____
_____ _____
_____ _____
_____ _____
_____ _____

PROJECT

PROJECT

PROJECT

MONTH:

Monday	Tuesday	Wednesday

Notes:

Thursday	Friday	Saturday	Sunday

Rituals for Living Challenge

This week, try to make someone laugh each day. If you don't know any jokes, find some good ones online, or employ other methods, such as tickling or doing a funny dance. Laughter is medicine.

TOP 3 GOALS THIS WEEK

TASKS
- MONTHLY PLAN
- INCOMPLETE FROM LAST WEEK
- LIFE DUTIES
- ★ STAR THE MOST IMPORTANT TASKS ★

Final task: schedule next week

NOW: PUT THESE TASKS & RITUALS IN YOUR CALENDAR, GO FORTH AND CONQUER!

MONTH:

	MONDAY	TUESDAY	WEDNESDAY
	INTENTION:	INTENTION:	INTENTION:
	MORNING RITUALS AND ACTIVITIES	MORNING RITUALS AND ACTIVITIES	MORNING RITUALS AND ACTIVITIES
8:00			
8:30			
9:00			
9:30			
10:00			
10:30			
11:00			
11:30			
	WHAT SHALL I BE FOCUSED ON?	WHERE IS MY ATTENTION GOING?	WHAT PERSPECTIVE DO I CHOOSE?
12:00			
12:30			
1:00			
1:30			
2:00			
2:30			
3:00			
3:30			
4:00			
4:30			
5:00			
5:30			
6:00			
	EVENING RITUALS AND ACTIVITIES	EVENING RITUALS AND ACTIVITIES	EVENING RITUALS AND ACTIVITIES
	I AM GRATEFUL FOR:	I AM GRATEFUL FOR:	I AM GRATEFUL FOR:

THURSDAY	FRIDAY	SATURDAY
INTENTION:	INTENTION:	INTENTION:
MORNING RITUALS AND ACTIVITIES	MORNING RITUALS AND ACTIVITIES	MORNING RITUALS AND ACTIVITIES
8:00	8:00	
8:30	8:30	
9:00	9:00	
9:30	9:30	EVENING RITUALS AND ACTIVITIES
10:00	10:00	
10:30	10:30	
11:00	11:00	
11:30	11:30	I AM GRATEFUL FOR:
HOW AM I SPENDING MY ENERGY?	HOW DO I AFFECT MY WORLD?	
12:00	12:00	
12:30	12:30	
1:00	1:00	
1:30	1:30	
2:00	2:00	SUNDAY
2:30	2:30	INTENTION:
3:00	3:00	
3:30	3:30	
4:00	4:00	MORNING RITUALS AND ACTIVITIES
4:30	4:30	
5:00	5:00	
5:30	5:30	
6:00	6:00	
EVENING RITUALS AND ACTIVITIES	EVENING RITUALS AND ACTIVITIES	
		EVENING RITUALS AND ACTIVITIES
I AM GRATEFUL FOR:	I AM GRATEFUL FOR:	
		I AM GRATEFUL FOR:

RITUALS FOR THRIVING

- ○ EXERCISE
- ○ MEDITATE / BREATHE
- ○ JOURNAL
- ○ DANCE
- ○ GO ON A DATE
- ○ CONNECT WITH NATURE
- ○ VISUALIZE
- ○ FAMILY TIME
- ○ COOK / EAT A HEALTHY MEAL
- ○ ORGANIZE MY SPACE / LIFE
- ○ GET RID OF THINGS I DON'T LOVE
- ○ BE WITH FRIENDS
- ○ PLAY
- ○ LET GO / FORGIVE
- ○ SING / MAKE MUSIC
- ○ CREATE ART
- ○ READ FOR ENJOYMENT
- ○ CONNECT / PRAY
- ○ CALL SOMEONE / WRITE A LETTER
- ○ STRETCH / DO YOGA
- ○ MASSAGE / EXCHANGE TOUCH
- ○ SERVE MY COMMUNITY

DREAM, EXPAND, RECORD, REFLECT:

FOCUS

Rituals for Living Challenge
This week, dance on at least three separate occasions. It doesn't matter whether you look good or have any skill. Dance is such a basic, primal form of expression, ritual, & release. Just put on music you love and let your body move.

TOP 3 GOALS THIS WEEK

TASKS
- MONTHLY PLAN
- INCOMPLETE FROM LAST WEEK
- LIFE DUTIES
- ★ STAR THE MOST IMPORTANT TASKS ★

Final task: schedule next week
NOW: PUT THESE TASKS & RITUALS IN YOUR CALENDAR, GO FORTH AND CONQUER!

MONTH:

	MONDAY	TUESDAY	WEDNESDAY
	INTENTION:	INTENTION:	INTENTION:
	MORNING RITUALS AND ACTIVITIES	MORNING RITUALS AND ACTIVITIES	MORNING RITUALS AND ACTIVITIES
8:00			
8:30			
9:00			
9:30			
10:00			
10:30			
11:00			
11:30			
	WHAT SHALL I BE FOCUSED ON?	WHERE IS MY ATTENTION GOING?	WHAT PERSPECTIVE DO I CHOOSE?
12:00			
12:30			
1:00			
1:30			
2:00			
2:30			
3:00			
3:30			
4:00			
4:30			
5:00			
5:30			
6:00			
	EVENING RITUALS AND ACTIVITIES	EVENING RITUALS AND ACTIVITIES	EVENING RITUALS AND ACTIVITIES
	I AM GRATEFUL FOR:	I AM GRATEFUL FOR:	I AM GRATEFUL FOR:

THURSDAY	FRIDAY	SATURDAY
INTENTION:	INTENTION:	INTENTION:
MORNING RITUALS AND ACTIVITIES	MORNING RITUALS AND ACTIVITIES	MORNING RITUALS AND ACTIVITIES
8:00	8:00	
8:30	8:30	
9:00	9:00	
9:30	9:30	EVENING RITUALS AND ACTIVITIES
10:00	10:00	
10:30	10:30	
11:00	11:00	
11:30	11:30	I AM GRATEFUL FOR:
HOW AM I SPENDING MY ENERGY?	HOW DO I AFFECT MY WORLD?	
12:00	12:00	
12:30	12:30	
1:00	1:00	
1:30	1:30	
2:00	2:00	SUNDAY
2:30	2:30	INTENTION:
3:00	3:00	
3:30	3:30	
4:00	4:00	MORNING RITUALS AND ACTIVITIES
4:30	4:30	
5:00	5:00	
5:30	5:30	
6:00	6:00	
EVENING RITUALS AND ACTIVITIES	EVENING RITUALS AND ACTIVITIES	
		EVENING RITUALS AND ACTIVITIES
I AM GRATEFUL FOR:	I AM GRATEFUL FOR:	
		I AM GRATEFUL FOR:

RITUALS FOR THRIVING

- ○ EXERCISE
- ○ MEDITATE / BREATHE
- ○ JOURNAL
- ○ DANCE
- ○ GO ON A DATE
- ○ CONNECT WITH NATURE
- ○ VISUALIZE
- ○ FAMILY TIME
- ○ COOK / EAT A HEALTHY MEAL
- ○ ORGANIZE MY SPACE / LIFE
- ○ GET RID OF THINGS I DON'T LOVE
- ○ BE WITH FRIENDS
- ○ PLAY
- ○ LET GO / FORGIVE
- ○ SING / MAKE MUSIC
- ○ CREATE ART
- ○ READ FOR ENJOYMENT
- ○ CONNECT / PRAY
- ○ CALL SOMEONE / WRITE A LETTER
- ○ STRETCH / DO YOGA
- ○ MASSAGE / EXCHANGE TOUCH
- ○ SERVE MY COMMUNITY

DREAM, EXPAND, RECORD, REFLECT:

FOCUS

Rituals for Living Challenge
Put your hands and/or bare feet directly on the earth each day. This is your home. This is the soil that sustains our plants and animals. Feel grounded & connected. Extra credit: connect away from civilization or sleep on the ground.

TOP 3 GOALS THIS WEEK

TASKS
- MONTHLY PLAN
- INCOMPLETE FROM LAST WEEK
- LIFE DUTIES
- ★ STAR THE MOST IMPORTANT TASKS ★

Final task: schedule next week
NOW: PUT THESE TASKS & RITUALS IN YOUR CALENDAR, GO FORTH AND CONQUER!

MONTH:

	MONDAY	TUESDAY	WEDNESDAY
	INTENTION:	INTENTION:	INTENTION:
	MORNING RITUALS AND ACTIVITIES	MORNING RITUALS AND ACTIVITIES	MORNING RITUALS AND ACTIVITIES
8:00			
8:30			
9:00			
9:30			
10:00			
10:30			
11:00			
11:30			
	WHAT SHALL I BE FOCUSED ON?	WHERE IS MY ATTENTION GOING?	WHAT PERSPECTIVE DO I CHOOSE?
12:00			
12:30			
1:00			
1:30			
2:00			
2:30			
3:00			
3:30			
4:00			
4:30			
5:00			
5:30			
6:00			
	EVENING RITUALS AND ACTIVITIES	EVENING RITUALS AND ACTIVITIES	EVENING RITUALS AND ACTIVITIES
	I AM GRATEFUL FOR:	I AM GRATEFUL FOR:	I AM GRATEFUL FOR:

RITUALS FOR THRIVING

- ○ EXERCISE
- ○ MEDITATE / BREATHE
- ○ JOURNAL
- ○ DANCE
- ○ GO ON A DATE
- ○ CONNECT WITH NATURE
- ○ VISUALIZE
- ○ FAMILY TIME
- ○ COOK / EAT A HEALTHY MEAL
- ○ ORGANIZE MY SPACE / LIFE
- ○ GET RID OF THINGS I DON'T LOVE
- ○ BE WITH FRIENDS
- ○ PLAY
- ○ LET GO / FORGIVE
- ○ SING / MAKE MUSIC
- ○ CREATE ART
- ○ READ FOR ENJOYMENT
- ○ CONNECT / PRAY
- ○ CALL SOMEONE / WRITE A LETTER
- ○ STRETCH / DO YOGA
- ○ MASSAGE / EXCHANGE TOUCH
- ○ SERVE MY COMMUNITY

THURSDAY	FRIDAY	SATURDAY
INTENTION:	INTENTION:	INTENTION:
MORNING RITUALS AND ACTIVITIES	MORNING RITUALS AND ACTIVITIES	MORNING RITUALS AND ACTIVITIES
8:00	8:00	
8:30	8:30	
9:00	9:00	
9:30	9:30	EVENING RITUALS AND ACTIVITIES
10:00	10:00	
10:30	10:30	
11:00	11:00	
11:30	11:30	I AM GRATEFUL FOR:
HOW AM I SPENDING MY ENERGY?	HOW DO I AFFECT MY WORLD?	
12:00	12:00	
12:30	12:30	
1:00	1:00	
1:30	1:30	
2:00	2:00	SUNDAY
2:30	2:30	INTENTION:
3:00	3:00	
3:30	3:30	
4:00	4:00	MORNING RITUALS AND ACTIVITIES
4:30	4:30	
5:00	5:00	
5:30	5:30	
6:00	6:00	
EVENING RITUALS AND ACTIVITIES	EVENING RITUALS AND ACTIVITIES	
		EVENING RITUALS AND ACTIVITIES
I AM GRATEFUL FOR:	I AM GRATEFUL FOR:	
		I AM GRATEFUL FOR:

DREAM, EXPAND, RECORD, REFLECT:

Rituals for Living Challenge

This week, clean something that has been needing to be cleaned. If there is nothing in your own space that needs cleaning, find something outside – some trash, some graffiti, etc. Honor your environment.

TOP 3 GOALS THIS WEEK

TASKS
- MONTHLY PLAN
- INCOMPLETE FROM LAST WEEK
- LIFE DUTIES
- ★ STAR THE MOST IMPORTANT TASKS ★

Final task: schedule next week

NOW: PUT THESE TASKS & RITUALS IN YOUR CALENDAR, GO FORTH AND CONQUER!

MONTH:

	MONDAY	TUESDAY	WEDNESDAY
	INTENTION:	INTENTION:	INTENTION:
	MORNING RITUALS AND ACTIVITIES	MORNING RITUALS AND ACTIVITIES	MORNING RITUALS AND ACTIVITIES
8:00			
8:30			
9:00			
9:30			
10:00			
10:30			
11:00			
11:30			
	WHAT SHALL I BE FOCUSED ON?	WHERE IS MY ATTENTION GOING?	WHAT PERSPECTIVE DO I CHOOSE?
12:00			
12:30			
1:00			
1:30			
2:00			
2:30			
3:00			
3:30			
4:00			
4:30			
5:00			
5:30			
6:00			
	EVENING RITUALS AND ACTIVITIES	EVENING RITUALS AND ACTIVITIES	EVENING RITUALS AND ACTIVITIES
	I AM GRATEFUL FOR:	I AM GRATEFUL FOR:	I AM GRATEFUL FOR:

THURSDAY	FRIDAY	SATURDAY	RITUALS FOR THRIVING
INTENTION:	INTENTION:	INTENTION:	○ EXERCISE
			○ MEDITATE / BREATHE
			○ JOURNAL
			○ DANCE
			○ GO ON A DATE
MORNING RITUALS AND ACTIVITIES	MORNING RITUALS AND ACTIVITIES	MORNING RITUALS AND ACTIVITIES	○ CONNECT WITH NATURE
			○ VISUALIZE
			○ FAMILY TIME
			○ COOK / EAT A HEALTHY MEAL
			○ ORGANIZE MY SPACE / LIFE
8:00	8:00		○ GET RID OF THINGS I DON'T LOVE
8:30	8:30		○ BE WITH FRIENDS
9:00	9:00		○ PLAY
9:30	9:30	EVENING RITUALS AND ACTIVITIES	○ LET GO / FORGIVE
10:00	10:00		○ SING / MAKE MUSIC
10:30	10:30		○ CREATE ART
11:00	11:00		○ READ FOR ENJOYMENT
11:30	11:30	I AM GRATEFUL FOR:	○ CONNECT / PRAY
HOW AM I SPENDING MY ENERGY?	HOW DO I AFFECT MY WORLD?		○ CALL SOMEONE / WRITE A LETTER
12:00	12:00		○ STRETCH / DO YOGA
12:30	12:30		○ MASSAGE / EXCHANGE TOUCH
1:00	1:00		○ SERVE MY COMMUNITY
1:30	1:30		
2:00	2:00	SUNDAY	DREAM, EXPAND, RECORD, REFLECT:
2:30	2:30	INTENTION:	
3:00	3:00		
3:30	3:30		
4:00	4:00	MORNING RITUALS AND ACTIVITIES	
4:30	4:30		
5:00	5:00		
5:30	5:30		
6:00	6:00		
EVENING RITUALS AND ACTIVITIES	EVENING RITUALS AND ACTIVITIES		
		EVENING RITUALS AND ACTIVITIES	
I AM GRATEFUL FOR:	I AM GRATEFUL FOR:		
		I AM GRATEFUL FOR:	

Rituals for Living Challenge

Every day, forgive yourself for everything. Catch yourself thinking you should be different or better, your past should be different, or you should be more like your idea of the perfect human. Forgive yourself, over and over.

TOP 3 GOALS THIS WEEK

TASKS
- MONTHLY PLAN
- INCOMPLETE FROM LAST WEEK
- LIFE DUTIES
- ★ STAR THE MOST IMPORTANT TASKS ★

Final task: schedule next week

NOW: PUT THESE TASKS & RITUALS IN YOUR CALENDAR, GO FORTH AND CONQUER!

MONTH:

	MONDAY	TUESDAY	WEDNESDAY
	INTENTION:	INTENTION:	INTENTION:
	MORNING RITUALS AND ACTIVITIES	MORNING RITUALS AND ACTIVITIES	MORNING RITUALS AND ACTIVITIES
8:00			
8:30			
9:00			
9:30			
10:00			
10:30			
11:00			
11:30			
	WHAT SHALL I BE FOCUSED ON?	WHERE IS MY ATTENTION GOING?	WHAT PERSPECTIVE DO I CHOOSE?
12:00			
12:30			
1:00			
1:30			
2:00			
2:30			
3:00			
3:30			
4:00			
4:30			
5:00			
5:30			
6:00			
	EVENING RITUALS AND ACTIVITIES	EVENING RITUALS AND ACTIVITIES	EVENING RITUALS AND ACTIVITIES
	I AM GRATEFUL FOR:	I AM GRATEFUL FOR:	I AM GRATEFUL FOR:

RITUALS FOR THRIVING

- ○ EXERCISE
- ○ MEDITATE / BREATHE
- ○ JOURNAL
- ○ DANCE
- ○ GO ON A DATE
- ○ CONNECT WITH NATURE
- ○ VISUALIZE
- ○ FAMILY TIME
- ○ COOK / EAT A HEALTHY MEAL
- ○ ORGANIZE MY SPACE / LIFE
- ○ GET RID OF THINGS I DON'T LOVE
- ○ BE WITH FRIENDS
- ○ PLAY
- ○ LET GO / FORGIVE
- ○ SING / MAKE MUSIC
- ○ CREATE ART
- ○ READ FOR ENJOYMENT
- ○ CONNECT / PRAY
- ○ CALL SOMEONE / WRITE A LETTER
- ○ STRETCH / DO YOGA
- ○ MASSAGE / EXCHANGE TOUCH
- ○ SERVE MY COMMUNITY

THURSDAY	FRIDAY	SATURDAY
INTENTION:	INTENTION:	INTENTION:
MORNING RITUALS AND ACTIVITIES	MORNING RITUALS AND ACTIVITIES	MORNING RITUALS AND ACTIVITIES
8:00	8:00	
8:30	8:30	
9:00	9:00	
9:30	9:30	EVENING RITUALS AND ACTIVITIES
10:00	10:00	
10:30	10:30	
11:00	11:00	
11:30	11:30	I AM GRATEFUL FOR:
HOW AM I SPENDING MY ENERGY?	HOW DO I AFFECT MY WORLD?	
12:00	12:00	
12:30	12:30	
1:00	1:00	
1:30	1:30	
2:00	2:00	**SUNDAY**
2:30	2:30	INTENTION:
3:00	3:00	
3:30	3:30	
4:00	4:00	MORNING RITUALS AND ACTIVITIES
4:30	4:30	
5:00	5:00	
5:30	5:30	
6:00	6:00	
EVENING RITUALS AND ACTIVITIES	EVENING RITUALS AND ACTIVITIES	
		EVENING RITUALS AND ACTIVITIES
I AM GRATEFUL FOR:	I AM GRATEFUL FOR:	
		I AM GRATEFUL FOR:

DREAM, EXPAND, RECORD, REFLECT:

Rituals for Living Challenge

This week, reduce your screen time. Instead of turning constantly to your cell phone, television, tablet, and computer, find other ways to be amused. Be satisfied with silence and natural objects.

TOP 3 GOALS THIS WEEK

TASKS
- MONTHLY PLAN
- INCOMPLETE FROM LAST WEEK
- LIFE DUTIES
- ★ STAR THE MOST IMPORTANT TASKS ★

Final task: schedule next week

NOW: PUT THESE TASKS & RITUALS IN YOUR CALENDAR, GO FORTH AND CONQUER!

MONTH:

	MONDAY	TUESDAY	WEDNESDAY
	INTENTION:	**INTENTION:**	**INTENTION:**
	MORNING RITUALS AND ACTIVITIES	**MORNING RITUALS AND ACTIVITIES**	**MORNING RITUALS AND ACTIVITIES**
8:00			
8:30			
9:00			
9:30			
10:00			
10:30			
11:00			
11:30			
	WHAT SHALL I BE FOCUSED ON?	WHERE IS MY ATTENTION GOING?	WHAT PERSPECTIVE DO I CHOOSE?
12:00			
12:30			
1:00			
1:30			
2:00			
2:30			
3:00			
3:30			
4:00			
4:30			
5:00			
5:30			
6:00			
	EVENING RITUALS AND ACTIVITIES	**EVENING RITUALS AND ACTIVITIES**	**EVENING RITUALS AND ACTIVITIES**
	I AM GRATEFUL FOR:	**I AM GRATEFUL FOR:**	**I AM GRATEFUL FOR:**

THURSDAY	FRIDAY	SATURDAY
INTENTION:	INTENTION:	INTENTION:
MORNING RITUALS AND ACTIVITIES	MORNING RITUALS AND ACTIVITIES	MORNING RITUALS AND ACTIVITIES
8:00	8:00	
8:30	8:30	
9:00	9:00	
9:30	9:30	EVENING RITUALS AND ACTIVITIES
10:00	10:00	
10:30	10:30	
11:00	11:00	
11:30	11:30	I AM GRATEFUL FOR:
HOW AM I SPENDING MY ENERGY?	HOW DO I AFFECT MY WORLD?	
12:00	12:00	
12:30	12:30	
1:00	1:00	
1:30	1:30	
2:00	2:00	**SUNDAY**
2:30	2:30	INTENTION:
3:00	3:00	
3:30	3:30	
4:00	4:00	MORNING RITUALS AND ACTIVITIES
4:30	4:30	
5:00	5:00	
5:30	5:30	
6:00	6:00	
EVENING RITUALS AND ACTIVITIES	EVENING RITUALS AND ACTIVITIES	
		EVENING RITUALS AND ACTIVITIES
I AM GRATEFUL FOR:	I AM GRATEFUL FOR:	
		I AM GRATEFUL FOR:

RITUALS FOR THRIVING

- ○ EXERCISE
- ○ MEDITATE / BREATHE
- ○ JOURNAL
- ○ DANCE
- ○ GO ON A DATE
- ○ CONNECT WITH NATURE
- ○ VISUALIZE
- ○ FAMILY TIME
- ○ COOK / EAT A HEALTHY MEAL
- ○ ORGANIZE MY SPACE / LIFE
- ○ GET RID OF THINGS I DON'T LOVE
- ○ BE WITH FRIENDS
- ○ PLAY
- ○ LET GO / FORGIVE
- ○ SING / MAKE MUSIC
- ○ CREATE ART
- ○ READ FOR ENJOYMENT
- ○ CONNECT / PRAY
- ○ CALL SOMEONE / WRITE A LETTER
- ○ STRETCH / DO YOGA
- ○ MASSAGE / EXCHANGE TOUCH
- ○ SERVE MY COMMUNITY

DREAM, EXPAND, RECORD, REFLECT:

Rituals for Living Challenge

This week, do something adventurous. It doesn't have to be bungee jumping. What does adventure mean to *you*?

TOP 3 GOALS THIS WEEK

TASKS
- MONTHLY PLAN
- INCOMPLETE FROM LAST WEEK
- LIFE DUTIES
- ★ STAR THE MOST IMPORTANT TASKS ★

Final task: schedule next week

NOW: PUT THESE TASKS & RITUALS IN YOUR CALENDAR, GO FORTH AND CONQUER!

MONTH:

	MONDAY	TUESDAY	WEDNESDAY
	INTENTION:	INTENTION:	INTENTION:
	MORNING RITUALS AND ACTIVITIES	MORNING RITUALS AND ACTIVITIES	MORNING RITUALS AND ACTIVITIES
8:00			
8:30			
9:00			
9:30			
10:00			
10:30			
11:00			
11:30			
	WHAT SHALL I BE FOCUSED ON?	WHERE IS MY ATTENTION GOING?	WHAT PERSPECTIVE DO I CHOOSE?
12:00			
12:30			
1:00			
1:30			
2:00			
2:30			
3:00			
3:30			
4:00			
4:30			
5:00			
5:30			
6:00			
	EVENING RITUALS AND ACTIVITIES	EVENING RITUALS AND ACTIVITIES	EVENING RITUALS AND ACTIVITIES
	I AM GRATEFUL FOR:	I AM GRATEFUL FOR:	I AM GRATEFUL FOR:

RITUALS FOR THRIVING

- ○ EXERCISE
- ○ MEDITATE / BREATHE
- ○ JOURNAL
- ○ DANCE
- ○ GO ON A DATE
- ○ CONNECT WITH NATURE
- ○ VISUALIZE
- ○ FAMILY TIME
- ○ COOK / EAT A HEALTHY MEAL
- ○ ORGANIZE MY SPACE / LIFE
- ○ GET RID OF THINGS I DON'T LOVE
- ○ BE WITH FRIENDS
- ○ PLAY
- ○ LET GO / FORGIVE
- ○ SING / MAKE MUSIC
- ○ CREATE ART
- ○ READ FOR ENJOYMENT
- ○ CONNECT / PRAY
- ○ CALL SOMEONE / WRITE A LETTER
- ○ STRETCH / DO YOGA
- ○ MASSAGE / EXCHANGE TOUCH
- ○ SERVE MY COMMUNITY

DREAM, EXPAND, RECORD, REFLECT:

THURSDAY	FRIDAY	SATURDAY
INTENTION:	INTENTION:	INTENTION:
MORNING RITUALS AND ACTIVITIES	MORNING RITUALS AND ACTIVITIES	MORNING RITUALS AND ACTIVITIES
8:00	8:00	
8:30	8:30	
9:00	9:00	
9:30	9:30	EVENING RITUALS AND ACTIVITIES
10:00	10:00	
10:30	10:30	
11:00	11:00	
11:30	11:30	I AM GRATEFUL FOR:
HOW AM I SPENDING MY ENERGY?	HOW DO I AFFECT MY WORLD?	
12:00	12:00	
12:30	12:30	
1:00	1:00	
1:30	1:30	
2:00	2:00	**SUNDAY**
2:30	2:30	INTENTION:
3:00	3:00	
3:30	3:30	
4:00	4:00	MORNING RITUALS AND ACTIVITIES
4:30	4:30	
5:00	5:00	
5:30	5:30	
6:00	6:00	
EVENING RITUALS AND ACTIVITIES	EVENING RITUALS AND ACTIVITIES	
		EVENING RITUALS AND ACTIVITIES
I AM GRATEFUL FOR:	I AM GRATEFUL FOR:	
		I AM GRATEFUL FOR:

Rituals for Living Challenge
Conserve your life energy. Use your ninja skills to perform with the least expense of your own energy. Be caring without giving energy away. Be efficient yet unattached, channel the available forces, choose the path of least resistance.

TOP 3 GOALS THIS WEEK

TASKS
- MONTHLY PLAN
- INCOMPLETE FROM LAST WEEK
- LIFE DUTIES
- ★ STAR THE MOST IMPORTANT TASKS ★

Final task: schedule next week

NOW: PUT THESE TASKS & RITUALS IN YOUR CALENDAR, GO FORTH AND CONQUER!

MONTH:

	MONDAY	TUESDAY	WEDNESDAY
	INTENTION:	INTENTION:	INTENTION:
	MORNING RITUALS AND ACTIVITIES	MORNING RITUALS AND ACTIVITIES	MORNING RITUALS AND ACTIVITIES
8:00			
8:30			
9:00			
9:30			
10:00			
10:30			
11:00			
11:30			
	WHAT SHALL I BE FOCUSED ON?	WHERE IS MY ATTENTION GOING?	WHAT PERSPECTIVE DO I CHOOSE?
12:00			
12:30			
1:00			
1:30			
2:00			
2:30			
3:00			
3:30			
4:00			
4:30			
5:00			
5:30			
6:00			
	EVENING RITUALS AND ACTIVITIES	EVENING RITUALS AND ACTIVITIES	EVENING RITUALS AND ACTIVITIES
	I AM GRATEFUL FOR:	I AM GRATEFUL FOR:	I AM GRATEFUL FOR:

THURSDAY	FRIDAY	SATURDAY
INTENTION:	INTENTION:	INTENTION:
MORNING RITUALS AND ACTIVITIES	MORNING RITUALS AND ACTIVITIES	MORNING RITUALS AND ACTIVITIES
8:00	8:00	
8:30	8:30	
9:00	9:00	
9:30	9:30	EVENING RITUALS AND ACTIVITIES
10:00	10:00	
10:30	10:30	
11:00	11:00	
11:30	11:30	I AM GRATEFUL FOR:
HOW AM I SPENDING MY ENERGY?	HOW DO I AFFECT MY WORLD?	
12:00	12:00	
12:30	12:30	
1:00	1:00	
1:30	1:30	
2:00	2:00	SUNDAY
2:30	2:30	INTENTION:
3:00	3:00	
3:30	3:30	
4:00	4:00	MORNING RITUALS AND ACTIVITIES
4:30	4:30	
5:00	5:00	
5:30	5:30	
6:00	6:00	
EVENING RITUALS AND ACTIVITIES	EVENING RITUALS AND ACTIVITIES	
		EVENING RITUALS AND ACTIVITIES
I AM GRATEFUL FOR:	I AM GRATEFUL FOR:	
		I AM GRATEFUL FOR:

RITUALS FOR THRIVING

- ○ EXERCISE
- ○ MEDITATE / BREATHE
- ○ JOURNAL
- ○ DANCE
- ○ GO ON A DATE
- ○ CONNECT WITH NATURE
- ○ VISUALIZE
- ○ FAMILY TIME
- ○ COOK / EAT A HEALTHY MEAL
- ○ ORGANIZE MY SPACE / LIFE
- ○ GET RID OF THINGS I DON'T LOVE
- ○ BE WITH FRIENDS
- ○ PLAY
- ○ LET GO / FORGIVE
- ○ SING / MAKE MUSIC
- ○ CREATE ART
- ○ READ FOR ENJOYMENT
- ○ CONNECT / PRAY
- ○ CALL SOMEONE / WRITE A LETTER
- ○ STRETCH / DO YOGA
- ○ MASSAGE / EXCHANGE TOUCH
- ○ SERVE MY COMMUNITY

DREAM, EXPAND, RECORD, REFLECT:

Rituals for Living Challenge

This week, beautify something you look at all the time. Hang a picture in your bathroom. Put a fresh coat of paint on the wall. Fill your space with flowers. Adorn your car with jewels. Put a crown on your dog.

TOP 3 GOALS THIS WEEK

TASKS
- MONTHLY PLAN
- INCOMPLETE FROM LAST WEEK
- LIFE DUTIES
- ★ STAR THE MOST IMPORTANT TASKS ★

Final task: schedule next week

NOW: PUT THESE TASKS & RITUALS IN YOUR CALENDAR, GO FORTH AND CONQUER!

MONTH:

	MONDAY	TUESDAY	WEDNESDAY
	INTENTION:	INTENTION:	INTENTION:
	MORNING RITUALS AND ACTIVITIES	MORNING RITUALS AND ACTIVITIES	MORNING RITUALS AND ACTIVITIES
8:00			
8:30			
9:00			
9:30			
10:00			
10:30			
11:00			
11:30			
	WHAT SHALL I BE FOCUSED ON?	WHERE IS MY ATTENTION GOING?	WHAT PERSPECTIVE DO I CHOOSE?
12:00			
12:30			
1:00			
1:30			
2:00			
2:30			
3:00			
3:30			
4:00			
4:30			
5:00			
5:30			
6:00			
	EVENING RITUALS AND ACTIVITIES	EVENING RITUALS AND ACTIVITIES	EVENING RITUALS AND ACTIVITIES
	I AM GRATEFUL FOR:	I AM GRATEFUL FOR:	I AM GRATEFUL FOR:

THURSDAY	FRIDAY	SATURDAY
INTENTION:	INTENTION:	INTENTION:
MORNING RITUALS AND ACTIVITIES	MORNING RITUALS AND ACTIVITIES	MORNING RITUALS AND ACTIVITIES
8:00	8:00	
8:30	8:30	
9:00	9:00	
9:30	9:30	EVENING RITUALS AND ACTIVITIES
10:00	10:00	
10:30	10:30	
11:00	11:00	
11:30	11:30	I AM GRATEFUL FOR:
HOW AM I SPENDING MY ENERGY?	HOW DO I AFFECT MY WORLD?	
12:00	12:00	
12:30	12:30	
1:00	1:00	
1:30	1:30	
2:00	2:00	SUNDAY
2:30	2:30	INTENTION:
3:00	3:00	
3:30	3:30	
4:00	4:00	MORNING RITUALS AND ACTIVITIES
4:30	4:30	
5:00	5:00	
5:30	5:30	
6:00	6:00	
EVENING RITUALS AND ACTIVITIES	EVENING RITUALS AND ACTIVITIES	
		EVENING RITUALS AND ACTIVITIES
I AM GRATEFUL FOR:	I AM GRATEFUL FOR:	
		I AM GRATEFUL FOR:

RITUALS FOR THRIVING

- ○ EXERCISE
- ○ MEDITATE / BREATHE
- ○ JOURNAL
- ○ DANCE
- ○ GO ON A DATE
- ○ CONNECT WITH NATURE
- ○ VISUALIZE
- ○ FAMILY TIME
- ○ COOK / EAT A HEALTHY MEAL
- ○ ORGANIZE MY SPACE / LIFE
- ○ GET RID OF THINGS I DON'T LOVE
- ○ BE WITH FRIENDS
- ○ PLAY
- ○ LET GO / FORGIVE
- ○ SING / MAKE MUSIC
- ○ CREATE ART
- ○ READ FOR ENJOYMENT
- ○ CONNECT / PRAY
- ○ CALL SOMEONE / WRITE A LETTER
- ○ STRETCH / DO YOGA
- ○ MASSAGE / EXCHANGE TOUCH
- ○ SERVE MY COMMUNITY

DREAM, EXPAND, RECORD, REFLECT:

Rituals for Living Challenge

This week, get some art supplies, tune in, and make a piece of art. It doesn't matter if you don't have any talent. Just connect with what's inside you and let it out. When it's done, frame it. Then hang it up or give it to someone.

TOP 3 GOALS THIS WEEK

TASKS
- MONTHLY PLAN
- INCOMPLETE FROM LAST WEEK
- LIFE DUTIES
- ★ STAR THE MOST IMPORTANT TASKS ★

Final task: schedule next week

NOW: PUT THESE TASKS & RITUALS IN YOUR CALENDAR, GO FORTH AND CONQUER!

MONTH:

	MONDAY	TUESDAY	WEDNESDAY
	INTENTION:	INTENTION:	INTENTION:
	MORNING RITUALS AND ACTIVITIES	MORNING RITUALS AND ACTIVITIES	MORNING RITUALS AND ACTIVITIES
8:00			
8:30			
9:00			
9:30			
10:00			
10:30			
11:00			
11:30			
	WHAT SHALL I BE FOCUSED ON?	WHERE IS MY ATTENTION GOING?	WHAT PERSPECTIVE DO I CHOOSE?
12:00			
12:30			
1:00			
1:30			
2:00			
2:30			
3:00			
3:30			
4:00			
4:30			
5:00			
5:30			
6:00			
	EVENING RITUALS AND ACTIVITIES	EVENING RITUALS AND ACTIVITIES	EVENING RITUALS AND ACTIVITIES
	I AM GRATEFUL FOR:	I AM GRATEFUL FOR:	I AM GRATEFUL FOR:

	THURSDAY	FRIDAY	SATURDAY
	INTENTION:	INTENTION:	INTENTION:
	MORNING RITUALS AND ACTIVITIES	MORNING RITUALS AND ACTIVITIES	MORNING RITUALS AND ACTIVITIES
8:00			
8:30			
9:00			
9:30			EVENING RITUALS AND ACTIVITIES
10:00			
10:30			
11:00			
11:30			I AM GRATEFUL FOR:
	HOW AM I SPENDING MY ENERGY?	HOW DO I AFFECT MY WORLD?	
12:00			
12:30			
1:00			
1:30			
2:00			SUNDAY
2:30			INTENTION:
3:00			
3:30			
4:00			MORNING RITUALS AND ACTIVITIES
4:30			
5:00			
5:30			
6:00			
	EVENING RITUALS AND ACTIVITIES	EVENING RITUALS AND ACTIVITIES	
			EVENING RITUALS AND ACTIVITIES
	I AM GRATEFUL FOR:	I AM GRATEFUL FOR:	
			I AM GRATEFUL FOR:

RITUALS FOR THRIVING

- ○ EXERCISE
- ○ MEDITATE / BREATHE
- ○ JOURNAL
- ○ DANCE
- ○ GO ON A DATE
- ○ CONNECT WITH NATURE
- ○ VISUALIZE
- ○ FAMILY TIME
- ○ COOK / EAT A HEALTHY MEAL
- ○ ORGANIZE MY SPACE / LIFE
- ○ GET RID OF THINGS I DON'T LOVE
- ○ BE WITH FRIENDS
- ○ PLAY
- ○ LET GO / FORGIVE
- ○ SING / MAKE MUSIC
- ○ CREATE ART
- ○ READ FOR ENJOYMENT
- ○ CONNECT / PRAY
- ○ CALL SOMEONE / WRITE A LETTER
- ○ STRETCH / DO YOGA
- ○ MASSAGE / EXCHANGE TOUCH
- ○ SERVE MY COMMUNITY

DREAM, EXPAND, RECORD, REFLECT:

Rituals for Living Challenge

This week, sit in front of a fire at least once. If you can't get to a fire, sit in front of as many candles as you can find. Imagine it entering you and burning up any negativity while filling your body and mind with light.

TOP 3 GOALS THIS WEEK

TASKS
- MONTHLY PLAN
- INCOMPLETE FROM LAST WEEK
- LIFE DUTIES
- ★ STAR THE MOST IMPORTANT TASKS ★

Final task: schedule next week

NOW: PUT THESE TASKS & RITUALS IN YOUR CALENDAR, GO FORTH AND CONQUER!

MONTH:

	MONDAY	TUESDAY	WEDNESDAY
	INTENTION:	INTENTION:	INTENTION:
	MORNING RITUALS AND ACTIVITIES	MORNING RITUALS AND ACTIVITIES	MORNING RITUALS AND ACTIVITIES
8:00			
8:30			
9:00			
9:30			
10:00			
10:30			
11:00			
11:30			
	WHAT SHALL I BE FOCUSED ON?	WHERE IS MY ATTENTION GOING?	WHAT PERSPECTIVE DO I CHOOSE?
12:00			
12:30			
1:00			
1:30			
2:00			
2:30			
3:00			
3:30			
4:00			
4:30			
5:00			
5:30			
6:00			
	EVENING RITUALS AND ACTIVITIES	EVENING RITUALS AND ACTIVITIES	EVENING RITUALS AND ACTIVITIES
	I AM GRATEFUL FOR:	I AM GRATEFUL FOR:	I AM GRATEFUL FOR:

RITUALS FOR THRIVING

- ○ EXERCISE
- ○ MEDITATE / BREATHE
- ○ JOURNAL
- ○ DANCE
- ○ GO ON A DATE
- ○ CONNECT WITH NATURE
- ○ VISUALIZE
- ○ FAMILY TIME
- ○ COOK / EAT A HEALTHY MEAL
- ○ ORGANIZE MY SPACE / LIFE
- ○ GET RID OF THINGS I DON'T LOVE
- ○ BE WITH FRIENDS
- ○ PLAY
- ○ LET GO / FORGIVE
- ○ SING / MAKE MUSIC
- ○ CREATE ART
- ○ READ FOR ENJOYMENT
- ○ CONNECT / PRAY
- ○ CALL SOMEONE / WRITE A LETTER
- ○ STRETCH / DO YOGA
- ○ MASSAGE / EXCHANGE TOUCH
- ○ SERVE MY COMMUNITY

THURSDAY	FRIDAY	SATURDAY
INTENTION:	INTENTION:	INTENTION:
MORNING RITUALS AND ACTIVITIES	MORNING RITUALS AND ACTIVITIES	MORNING RITUALS AND ACTIVITIES
8:00	8:00	
8:30	8:30	
9:00	9:00	
9:30	9:30	EVENING RITUALS AND ACTIVITIES
10:00	10:00	
10:30	10:30	
11:00	11:00	
11:30	11:30	I AM GRATEFUL FOR:
HOW AM I SPENDING MY ENERGY?	HOW DO I AFFECT MY WORLD?	
12:00	12:00	
12:30	12:30	
1:00	1:00	
1:30	1:30	
2:00	2:00	**SUNDAY**
2:30	2:30	INTENTION:
3:00	3:00	
3:30	3:30	MORNING RITUALS AND ACTIVITIES
4:00	4:00	
4:30	4:30	
5:00	5:00	
5:30	5:30	
6:00	6:00	
EVENING RITUALS AND ACTIVITIES	EVENING RITUALS AND ACTIVITIES	
		EVENING RITUALS AND ACTIVITIES
I AM GRATEFUL FOR:	I AM GRATEFUL FOR:	
		I AM GRATEFUL FOR:

DREAM, EXPAND, RECORD, REFLECT:

Rituals for Living Challenge

This week, get into a natural body of water. (Or at least take 2 long baths.) As you get in set an intention, such as: to be de-stressed, to go with the flow, to have your energy neutralized, to be cleansed, or to be put back in sync with nature.

TOP 3 GOALS THIS WEEK

TASKS
- MONTHLY PLAN
- INCOMPLETE FROM LAST WEEK
- LIFE DUTIES
- ★ STAR THE MOST IMPORTANT TASKS ★

Final task: schedule next week

NOW: PUT THESE TASKS & RITUALS IN YOUR CALENDAR, GO FORTH AND CONQUER!

MONTH:

	MONDAY	TUESDAY	WEDNESDAY
	INTENTION:	INTENTION:	INTENTION:
	MORNING RITUALS AND ACTIVITIES	MORNING RITUALS AND ACTIVITIES	MORNING RITUALS AND ACTIVITIES
8:00			
8:30			
9:00			
9:30			
10:00			
10:30			
11:00			
11:30			
	WHAT SHALL I BE FOCUSED ON?	WHERE IS MY ATTENTION GOING?	WHAT PERSPECTIVE DO I CHOOSE?
12:00			
12:30			
1:00			
1:30			
2:00			
2:30			
3:00			
3:30			
4:00			
4:30			
5:00			
5:30			
6:00			
	EVENING RITUALS AND ACTIVITIES	EVENING RITUALS AND ACTIVITIES	EVENING RITUALS AND ACTIVITIES
	I AM GRATEFUL FOR:	I AM GRATEFUL FOR:	I AM GRATEFUL FOR:

THURSDAY	FRIDAY	SATURDAY
INTENTION:	INTENTION:	INTENTION:
MORNING RITUALS AND ACTIVITIES	MORNING RITUALS AND ACTIVITIES	MORNING RITUALS AND ACTIVITIES
8:00	8:00	
8:30	8:30	
9:00	9:00	
9:30	9:30	EVENING RITUALS AND ACTIVITIES
10:00	10:00	
10:30	10:30	
11:00	11:00	
11:30	11:30	I AM GRATEFUL FOR:
HOW AM I SPENDING MY ENERGY?	HOW DO I AFFECT MY WORLD?	
12:00	12:00	
12:30	12:30	
1:00	1:00	
1:30	1:30	
2:00	2:00	SUNDAY
2:30	2:30	INTENTION:
3:00	3:00	
3:30	3:30	
4:00	4:00	MORNING RITUALS AND ACTIVITIES
4:30	4:30	
5:00	5:00	
5:30	5:30	
6:00	6:00	
EVENING RITUALS AND ACTIVITIES	EVENING RITUALS AND ACTIVITIES	
		EVENING RITUALS AND ACTIVITIES
I AM GRATEFUL FOR:	I AM GRATEFUL FOR:	
		I AM GRATEFUL FOR:

RITUALS FOR THRIVING

- ○ EXERCISE
- ○ MEDITATE / BREATHE
- ○ JOURNAL
- ○ DANCE
- ○ GO ON A DATE
- ○ CONNECT WITH NATURE
- ○ VISUALIZE
- ○ FAMILY TIME
- ○ COOK / EAT A HEALTHY MEAL
- ○ ORGANIZE MY SPACE / LIFE
- ○ GET RID OF THINGS I DON'T LOVE
- ○ BE WITH FRIENDS
- ○ PLAY
- ○ LET GO / FORGIVE
- ○ SING / MAKE MUSIC
- ○ CREATE ART
- ○ READ FOR ENJOYMENT
- ○ CONNECT / PRAY
- ○ CALL SOMEONE / WRITE A LETTER
- ○ STRETCH / DO YOGA
- ○ MASSAGE / EXCHANGE TOUCH
- ○ SERVE MY COMMUNITY

DREAM, EXPAND, RECORD, REFLECT:

Rituals for Living Challenge

This week, at least three times, lie on your back outdoors and look up at the sky. Feel the vastness that you're part of.

TOP 3 GOALS THIS WEEK

TASKS
- MONTHLY PLAN
- INCOMPLETE FROM LAST WEEK
- LIFE DUTIES
- ★ STAR THE MOST IMPORTANT TASKS ★

Final task: schedule next week

NOW: PUT THESE TASKS & RITUALS IN YOUR CALENDAR, GO FORTH AND CONQUER!

MONTH:

	MONDAY	TUESDAY	WEDNESDAY
	INTENTION:	INTENTION:	INTENTION:
	MORNING RITUALS AND ACTIVITIES	MORNING RITUALS AND ACTIVITIES	MORNING RITUALS AND ACTIVITIES
8:00			
8:30			
9:00			
9:30			
10:00			
10:30			
11:00			
11:30			
	WHAT SHALL I BE FOCUSED ON?	WHERE IS MY ATTENTION GOING?	WHAT PERSPECTIVE DO I CHOOSE?
12:00			
12:30			
1:00			
1:30			
2:00			
2:30			
3:00			
3:30			
4:00			
4:30			
5:00			
5:30			
6:00			
	EVENING RITUALS AND ACTIVITIES	EVENING RITUALS AND ACTIVITIES	EVENING RITUALS AND ACTIVITIES
	I AM GRATEFUL FOR:	I AM GRATEFUL FOR:	I AM GRATEFUL FOR:

	THURSDAY	FRIDAY	SATURDAY
	INTENTION:	INTENTION:	INTENTION:
	MORNING RITUALS AND ACTIVITIES	MORNING RITUALS AND ACTIVITIES	MORNING RITUALS AND ACTIVITIES
8:00			
8:30			
9:00			
9:30			EVENING RITUALS AND ACTIVITIES
10:00			
10:30			
11:00			
11:30			I AM GRATEFUL FOR:
	HOW AM I SPENDING MY ENERGY?	HOW DO I AFFECT MY WORLD?	
12:00			
12:30			
1:00			
1:30			
2:00			SUNDAY
2:30			INTENTION:
3:00			
3:30			
4:00			MORNING RITUALS AND ACTIVITIES
4:30			
5:00			
5:30			
6:00			
	EVENING RITUALS AND ACTIVITIES	EVENING RITUALS AND ACTIVITIES	
			EVENING RITUALS AND ACTIVITIES
	I AM GRATEFUL FOR:	I AM GRATEFUL FOR:	
			I AM GRATEFUL FOR:

RITUALS FOR THRIVING

- ○ EXERCISE
- ○ MEDITATE / BREATHE
- ○ JOURNAL
- ○ DANCE
- ○ GO ON A DATE
- ○ CONNECT WITH NATURE
- ○ VISUALIZE
- ○ FAMILY TIME
- ○ COOK / EAT A HEALTHY MEAL
- ○ ORGANIZE MY SPACE / LIFE
- ○ GET RID OF THINGS I DON'T LOVE
- ○ BE WITH FRIENDS
- ○ PLAY
- ○ LET GO / FORGIVE
- ○ SING / MAKE MUSIC
- ○ CREATE ART
- ○ READ FOR ENJOYMENT
- ○ CONNECT / PRAY
- ○ CALL SOMEONE / WRITE A LETTER
- ○ STRETCH / DO YOGA
- ○ MASSAGE / EXCHANGE TOUCH
- ○ SERVE MY COMMUNITY

DREAM, EXPAND, RECORD, REFLECT:

It's time to reflect on the past quarter and decide what you want to refine as you move forward.

1. What was your biggest time and/or energy waster in the past quarter?

_____
_____

2. Which activities and rituals yielded the biggest "return" for you (either tangible or intangible) in the past quarter?

_____
_____

3. Is there anything you've been procrastinating over the past quarter?

_____
_____

4. Which of the items from the Rituals for Thriving list did you never do but would like to?

_____
_____

5. If anything happened in the last quarter that you would like to *reframe* (i.e., change the story you tell yourself and others about it, so as to hold it in a more positive light), please write how you intend to reframe it.

_____
_____
_____

6. What has been infringing on your happiness, health, or productivity in the past quarter that you intend to let go of in the coming quarter?

_____
_____
_____

NOW, use these answers to shape your focus and refine your
thoughts and behaviors in the coming quarter!

Quarter Three Breakdown

1. Get into your *ritual for planning* space. Do whatever you do to tune in (light a candle, take a breath, go to a peaceful spot, set an intention, etc.).

2. Look back at your What I Will Accomplish This Year list, and find all the projects that will be occurring in the coming quarter. Write each one in the table below and mark the appropriate month number(s) for the month(s) in which it will taking place. There is space at the top of the Month column to write abbreviations of the names of the months above ① ② and ③.

Project	Month		
	①	②	③
	①	②	③
	①	②	③
	①	②	③
	①	②	③
	①	②	③
	①	②	③
	①	②	③
	①	②	③
	①	②	③
	①	②	③
	①	②	③
	①	②	③
	①	②	③
	①	②	③
	①	②	③
	①	②	③
	①	②	③
	①	②	③
	①	②	③
	①	②	③
	①	②	③

Month:

1. Get into your *ritual for planning* space.

2. Gather the projects from the Quarterly Breakdown that pertain to this month and write each one on a PROJECT line below.

3. Under the project name, enter all of the tasks that are involved in the project. Each of these tasks must be a single action step, so that it can be put into your calendar and when you see it, no analysis needs to occur – you know exactly what to do.

PROJECT

PROJECT

PROJECT

_____   _____
_____   _____
_____   _____
_____   _____
_____   _____
_____   _____
_____   _____
_____   _____

PROJECT

_____   _____
_____   _____
_____   _____
_____   _____
_____   _____
_____   _____
_____   _____
_____   _____

PROJECT

_____   _____
_____   _____
_____   _____
_____   _____
_____   _____
_____   _____
_____   _____
_____   _____

MONTH:

Monday	Tuesday	Wednesday

Notes:

Thursday	Friday	Saturday	Sunday

Month:

1. Get into your *ritual for planning* space.

2. Gather the projects from the Quarterly Breakdown that pertain to this month and write each one on a PROJECT line below.

3. Under the project name, enter all of the tasks that are involved in the project. Each of these tasks must be a single action step, so that it can be put into your calendar and when you see it, no analysis needs to occur – you know exactly what to do.

PROJECT

_____

PROJECT

PROJECT

PROJECT

PROJECT

MONTH:

Monday	Tuesday	Wednesday

Notes:

Thursday	Friday	Saturday	Sunday

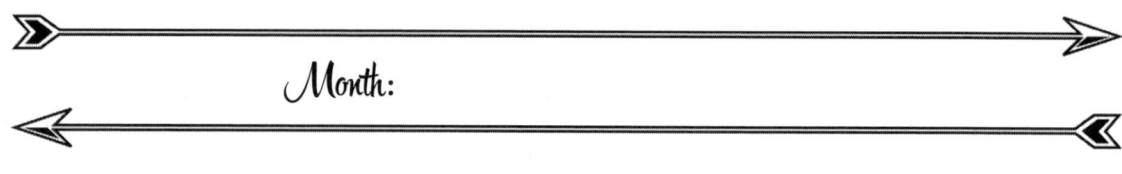

Month:

1. Get into your *ritual for planning* space.

2. Gather the projects from the Quarterly Breakdown that pertain to this month and write each one on a PROJECT line below.

3. Under the project name, enter all of the tasks that are involved in the project. Each of these tasks must be a single action step, so that it can be put into your calendar and when you see it, no analysis needs to occur – you know exactly what to do.

PROJECT

PROJECT

PROJECT

PROJECT

PROJECT

MONTH:

Monday	Tuesday	Wednesday

Notes:

Thursday	Friday	Saturday	Sunday

Rituals for Living Challenge

This week, plant a seed, start a cutting, or buy a new plant. Make a commitment to take good care of it. Plants clean the air, add beauty to our surroundings, and bring life to our living space.

TOP 3 GOALS THIS WEEK

TASKS
- MONTHLY PLAN
- INCOMPLETE FROM LAST WEEK
- LIFE DUTIES
- ★ STAR THE MOST IMPORTANT TASKS ★

Final task: schedule next week

NOW: PUT THESE TASKS & RITUALS IN YOUR CALENDAR, GO FORTH AND CONQUER!

MONTH:

	MONDAY	TUESDAY	WEDNESDAY
	INTENTION:	INTENTION:	INTENTION:
	MORNING RITUALS AND ACTIVITIES	**MORNING RITUALS AND ACTIVITIES**	**MORNING RITUALS AND ACTIVITIES**
8:00			
8:30			
9:00			
9:30			
10:00			
10:30			
11:00			
11:30			
	WHAT SHALL I BE FOCUSED ON?	WHERE IS MY ATTENTION GOING?	WHAT PERSPECTIVE DO I CHOOSE?
12:00			
12:30			
1:00			
1:30			
2:00			
2:30			
3:00			
3:30			
4:00			
4:30			
5:00			
5:30			
6:00			
	EVENING RITUALS AND ACTIVITIES	**EVENING RITUALS AND ACTIVITIES**	**EVENING RITUALS AND ACTIVITIES**
	I AM GRATEFUL FOR:	**I AM GRATEFUL FOR:**	**I AM GRATEFUL FOR:**

RITUALS FOR THRIVING

- ○ EXERCISE
- ○ MEDITATE / BREATHE
- ○ JOURNAL
- ○ DANCE
- ○ GO ON A DATE
- ○ CONNECT WITH NATURE
- ○ VISUALIZE
- ○ FAMILY TIME
- ○ COOK / EAT A HEALTHY MEAL
- ○ ORGANIZE MY SPACE / LIFE
- ○ GET RID OF THINGS I DON'T LOVE
- ○ BE WITH FRIENDS
- ○ PLAY
- ○ LET GO / FORGIVE
- ○ SING / MAKE MUSIC
- ○ CREATE ART
- ○ READ FOR ENJOYMENT
- ○ CONNECT / PRAY
- ○ CALL SOMEONE / WRITE A LETTER
- ○ STRETCH / DO YOGA
- ○ MASSAGE / EXCHANGE TOUCH
- ○ SERVE MY COMMUNITY

THURSDAY	FRIDAY	SATURDAY
INTENTION:	INTENTION:	INTENTION:
MORNING RITUALS AND ACTIVITIES	MORNING RITUALS AND ACTIVITIES	MORNING RITUALS AND ACTIVITIES
8:00	8:00	
8:30	8:30	
9:00	9:00	
9:30	9:30	EVENING RITUALS AND ACTIVITIES
10:00	10:00	
10:30	10:30	
11:00	11:00	
11:30	11:30	I AM GRATEFUL FOR:
HOW AM I SPENDING MY ENERGY?	HOW DO I AFFECT MY WORLD?	
12:00	12:00	
12:30	12:30	
1:00	1:00	
1:30	1:30	
2:00	2:00	SUNDAY
2:30	2:30	INTENTION:
3:00	3:00	
3:30	3:30	
4:00	4:00	MORNING RITUALS AND ACTIVITIES
4:30	4:30	
5:00	5:00	
5:30	5:30	
6:00	6:00	
EVENING RITUALS AND ACTIVITIES	EVENING RITUALS AND ACTIVITIES	
		EVENING RITUALS AND ACTIVITIES
I AM GRATEFUL FOR:	I AM GRATEFUL FOR:	
		I AM GRATEFUL FOR:

DREAM, EXPAND, RECORD, REFLECT:

FOCUS

Rituals for Living Challenge
This week, consume as little sweetener as possible - including white sugar, corn syrup, agave nectar, honey, maple syrup, fruit juice, rice syrup, evaporated cane juice, etc. Humans eat more sweetener than ever before. Break your addiction.

TOP 3 GOALS THIS WEEK

TASKS
- MONTHLY PLAN
- INCOMPLETE FROM LAST WEEK
- LIFE DUTIES
- ★ STAR THE MOST IMPORTANT TASKS ★

Final task: schedule next week

NOW: PUT THESE TASKS & RITUALS IN YOUR CALENDAR, GO FORTH AND CONQUER!

MONTH:

	MONDAY	TUESDAY	WEDNESDAY
	INTENTION:	**INTENTION:**	**INTENTION:**
	MORNING RITUALS AND ACTIVITIES	**MORNING RITUALS AND ACTIVITIES**	**MORNING RITUALS AND ACTIVITIES**
8:00			
8:30			
9:00			
9:30			
10:00			
10:30			
11:00			
11:30			
	WHAT SHALL I BE FOCUSED ON?	**WHERE IS MY ATTENTION GOING?**	**WHAT PERSPECTIVE DO I CHOOSE?**
12:00			
12:30			
1:00			
1:30			
2:00			
2:30			
3:00			
3:30			
4:00			
4:30			
5:00			
5:30			
6:00			
	EVENING RITUALS AND ACTIVITIES	**EVENING RITUALS AND ACTIVITIES**	**EVENING RITUALS AND ACTIVITIES**
	I AM GRATEFUL FOR:	**I AM GRATEFUL FOR:**	**I AM GRATEFUL FOR:**

RITUALS FOR THRIVING

- ○ EXERCISE
- ○ MEDITATE / BREATHE
- ○ JOURNAL
- ○ DANCE
- ○ GO ON A DATE
- ○ CONNECT WITH NATURE
- ○ VISUALIZE
- ○ FAMILY TIME
- ○ COOK / EAT A HEALTHY MEAL
- ○ ORGANIZE MY SPACE / LIFE
- ○ GET RID OF THINGS I DON'T LOVE
- ○ BE WITH FRIENDS
- ○ PLAY
- ○ LET GO / FORGIVE
- ○ SING / MAKE MUSIC
- ○ CREATE ART
- ○ READ FOR ENJOYMENT
- ○ CONNECT / PRAY
- ○ CALL SOMEONE / WRITE A LETTER
- ○ STRETCH / DO YOGA
- ○ MASSAGE / EXCHANGE TOUCH
- ○ SERVE MY COMMUNITY

THURSDAY	FRIDAY	SATURDAY
INTENTION:	INTENTION:	INTENTION:
MORNING RITUALS AND ACTIVITIES	MORNING RITUALS AND ACTIVITIES	MORNING RITUALS AND ACTIVITIES
8:00	8:00	
8:30	8:30	
9:00	9:00	
9:30	9:30	EVENING RITUALS AND ACTIVITIES
10:00	10:00	
10:30	10:30	
11:00	11:00	
11:30	11:30	I AM GRATEFUL FOR:
HOW AM I SPENDING MY ENERGY?	HOW DO I AFFECT MY WORLD?	
12:00	12:00	
12:30	12:30	
1:00	1:00	
1:30	1:30	
2:00	2:00	SUNDAY
2:30	2:30	INTENTION:
3:00	3:00	
3:30	3:30	
4:00	4:00	MORNING RITUALS AND ACTIVITIES
4:30	4:30	
5:00	5:00	
5:30	5:30	
6:00	6:00	
EVENING RITUALS AND ACTIVITIES	EVENING RITUALS AND ACTIVITIES	
		EVENING RITUALS AND ACTIVITIES
I AM GRATEFUL FOR:	I AM GRATEFUL FOR:	
		I AM GRATEFUL FOR:

DREAM, EXPAND, RECORD, REFLECT:

Rituals for Living Challenge
This week is a self-lovefest. Apologize for the ways you've mistreated, criticized, neglected, & withheld love from yourself. Tell yourself, "I love you, [name]." Be sweet to yourself. Take yourself on a date. Cherish yourself, honor yourself.

TOP 3 GOALS THIS WEEK

TASKS
- MONTHLY PLAN
- INCOMPLETE FROM LAST WEEK
- LIFE DUTIES
- ★ STAR THE MOST IMPORTANT TASKS ★

Final task: schedule next week

NOW: PUT THESE TASKS & RITUALS IN YOUR CALENDAR, GO FORTH AND CONQUER!

MONTH:

	MONDAY	TUESDAY	WEDNESDAY
	INTENTION:	INTENTION:	INTENTION:
	MORNING RITUALS AND ACTIVITIES	MORNING RITUALS AND ACTIVITIES	MORNING RITUALS AND ACTIVITIES
8:00			
8:30			
9:00			
9:30			
10:00			
10:30			
11:00			
11:30			
	WHAT SHALL I BE FOCUSED ON?	WHERE IS MY ATTENTION GOING?	WHAT PERSPECTIVE DO I CHOOSE?
12:00			
12:30			
1:00			
1:30			
2:00			
2:30			
3:00			
3:30			
4:00			
4:30			
5:00			
5:30			
6:00			
	EVENING RITUALS AND ACTIVITIES	EVENING RITUALS AND ACTIVITIES	EVENING RITUALS AND ACTIVITIES
	I AM GRATEFUL FOR:	I AM GRATEFUL FOR:	I AM GRATEFUL FOR:

RITUALS FOR THRIVING

- ○ EXERCISE
- ○ MEDITATE / BREATHE
- ○ JOURNAL
- ○ DANCE
- ○ GO ON A DATE
- ○ CONNECT WITH NATURE
- ○ VISUALIZE
- ○ FAMILY TIME
- ○ COOK / EAT A HEALTHY MEAL
- ○ ORGANIZE MY SPACE / LIFE
- ○ GET RID OF THINGS I DON'T LOVE
- ○ BE WITH FRIENDS
- ○ PLAY
- ○ LET GO / FORGIVE
- ○ SING / MAKE MUSIC
- ○ CREATE ART
- ○ READ FOR ENJOYMENT
- ○ CONNECT / PRAY
- ○ CALL SOMEONE / WRITE A LETTER
- ○ STRETCH / DO YOGA
- ○ MASSAGE / EXCHANGE TOUCH
- ○ SERVE MY COMMUNITY

THURSDAY	FRIDAY	SATURDAY
INTENTION:	INTENTION:	INTENTION:
MORNING RITUALS AND ACTIVITIES	MORNING RITUALS AND ACTIVITIES	MORNING RITUALS AND ACTIVITIES
8:00	8:00	
8:30	8:30	
9:00	9:00	
9:30	9:30	EVENING RITUALS AND ACTIVITIES
10:00	10:00	
10:30	10:30	
11:00	11:00	
11:30	11:30	I AM GRATEFUL FOR:
HOW AM I SPENDING MY ENERGY?	HOW DO I AFFECT MY WORLD?	
12:00	12:00	
12:30	12:30	
1:00	1:00	
1:30	1:30	
2:00	2:00	SUNDAY
2:30	2:30	INTENTION:
3:00	3:00	
3:30	3:30	
4:00	4:00	MORNING RITUALS AND ACTIVITIES
4:30	4:30	
5:00	5:00	
5:30	5:30	
6:00	6:00	
EVENING RITUALS AND ACTIVITIES	EVENING RITUALS AND ACTIVITIES	
		EVENING RITUALS AND ACTIVITIES
I AM GRATEFUL FOR:	I AM GRATEFUL FOR:	
		I AM GRATEFUL FOR:

DREAM, EXPAND, RECORD, REFLECT:

Rituals for Living Challenge

This week, at least twice, invite someone to share a meal with you.
Extra credit: cook the meal yourself.

TOP 3 GOALS THIS WEEK

TASKS
- MONTHLY PLAN
- INCOMPLETE FROM LAST WEEK
- LIFE DUTIES
- ★ STAR THE MOST IMPORTANT TASKS ★

Final task: schedule next week

NOW: PUT THESE TASKS & RITUALS IN YOUR CALENDAR, GO FORTH AND CONQUER!

MONTH:

	MONDAY	TUESDAY	WEDNESDAY
	INTENTION:	INTENTION:	INTENTION:
	MORNING RITUALS AND ACTIVITIES	MORNING RITUALS AND ACTIVITIES	MORNING RITUALS AND ACTIVITIES
8:00			
8:30			
9:00			
9:30			
10:00			
10:30			
11:00			
11:30			
	WHAT SHALL I BE FOCUSED ON?	WHERE IS MY ATTENTION GOING?	WHAT PERSPECTIVE DO I CHOOSE?
12:00			
12:30			
1:00			
1:30			
2:00			
2:30			
3:00			
3:30			
4:00			
4:30			
5:00			
5:30			
6:00			
	EVENING RITUALS AND ACTIVITIES	EVENING RITUALS AND ACTIVITIES	EVENING RITUALS AND ACTIVITIES
	I AM GRATEFUL FOR:	I AM GRATEFUL FOR:	I AM GRATEFUL FOR:

THURSDAY	FRIDAY	SATURDAY
INTENTION:	INTENTION:	INTENTION:
MORNING RITUALS AND ACTIVITIES	MORNING RITUALS AND ACTIVITIES	MORNING RITUALS AND ACTIVITIES
8:00	8:00	
8:30	8:30	
9:00	9:00	
9:30	9:30	EVENING RITUALS AND ACTIVITIES
10:00	10:00	
10:30	10:30	
11:00	11:00	
11:30	11:30	I AM GRATEFUL FOR:
HOW AM I SPENDING MY ENERGY?	HOW DO I AFFECT MY WORLD?	
12:00	12:00	
12:30	12:30	
1:00	1:00	
1:30	1:30	
2:00	2:00	SUNDAY
2:30	2:30	INTENTION:
3:00	3:00	
3:30	3:30	
4:00	4:00	MORNING RITUALS AND ACTIVITIES
4:30	4:30	
5:00	5:00	
5:30	5:30	
6:00	6:00	
EVENING RITUALS AND ACTIVITIES	EVENING RITUALS AND ACTIVITIES	
		EVENING RITUALS AND ACTIVITIES
I AM GRATEFUL FOR:	I AM GRATEFUL FOR:	
		I AM GRATEFUL FOR:

RITUALS FOR THRIVING

- ○ EXERCISE
- ○ MEDITATE / BREATHE
- ○ JOURNAL
- ○ DANCE
- ○ GO ON A DATE
- ○ CONNECT WITH NATURE
- ○ VISUALIZE
- ○ FAMILY TIME
- ○ COOK / EAT A HEALTHY MEAL
- ○ ORGANIZE MY SPACE / LIFE
- ○ GET RID OF THINGS I DON'T LOVE
- ○ BE WITH FRIENDS
- ○ PLAY
- ○ LET GO / FORGIVE
- ○ SING / MAKE MUSIC
- ○ CREATE ART
- ○ READ FOR ENJOYMENT
- ○ CONNECT / PRAY
- ○ CALL SOMEONE / WRITE A LETTER
- ○ STRETCH / DO YOGA
- ○ MASSAGE / EXCHANGE TOUCH
- ○ SERVE MY COMMUNITY

DREAM, EXPAND, RECORD, REFLECT:

FOCUS

Rituals for Living Challenge
This week, at least once, give yourself a foot massage for at least ten minutes per foot. Use some oil or lotion. If you don't have feet or can't reach them, massage another part of your body — or, for extra credit — your whole body.

TOP 3 GOALS THIS WEEK

TASKS
- MONTHLY PLAN
- INCOMPLETE FROM LAST WEEK
- LIFE DUTIES
- ★ STAR THE MOST IMPORTANT TASKS ★

Final task: schedule next week

NOW: PUT THESE TASKS & RITUALS IN YOUR CALENDAR, GO FORTH AND CONQUER!

MONTH:

	MONDAY	TUESDAY	WEDNESDAY
	INTENTION:	INTENTION:	INTENTION:
	MORNING RITUALS AND ACTIVITIES	MORNING RITUALS AND ACTIVITIES	MORNING RITUALS AND ACTIVITIES
8:00			
8:30			
9:00			
9:30			
10:00			
10:30			
11:00			
11:30			
	WHAT SHALL I BE FOCUSED ON?	WHERE IS MY ATTENTION GOING?	WHAT PERSPECTIVE DO I CHOOSE?
12:00			
12:30			
1:00			
1:30			
2:00			
2:30			
3:00			
3:30			
4:00			
4:30			
5:00			
5:30			
6:00			
	EVENING RITUALS AND ACTIVITIES	EVENING RITUALS AND ACTIVITIES	EVENING RITUALS AND ACTIVITIES
	I AM GRATEFUL FOR:	I AM GRATEFUL FOR:	I AM GRATEFUL FOR:

RITUALS FOR THRIVING

- ○ EXERCISE
- ○ MEDITATE / BREATHE
- ○ JOURNAL
- ○ DANCE
- ○ GO ON A DATE
- ○ CONNECT WITH NATURE
- ○ VISUALIZE
- ○ FAMILY TIME
- ○ COOK / EAT A HEALTHY MEAL
- ○ ORGANIZE MY SPACE / LIFE
- ○ GET RID OF THINGS I DON'T LOVE
- ○ BE WITH FRIENDS
- ○ PLAY
- ○ LET GO / FORGIVE
- ○ SING / MAKE MUSIC
- ○ CREATE ART
- ○ READ FOR ENJOYMENT
- ○ CONNECT / PRAY
- ○ CALL SOMEONE / WRITE A LETTER
- ○ STRETCH / DO YOGA
- ○ MASSAGE / EXCHANGE TOUCH
- ○ SERVE MY COMMUNITY

THURSDAY	FRIDAY	SATURDAY
INTENTION:	INTENTION:	INTENTION:
MORNING RITUALS AND ACTIVITIES	MORNING RITUALS AND ACTIVITIES	MORNING RITUALS AND ACTIVITIES
8:00	8:00	
8:30	8:30	
9:00	9:00	
9:30	9:30	EVENING RITUALS AND ACTIVITIES
10:00	10:00	
10:30	10:30	
11:00	11:00	
11:30	11:30	I AM GRATEFUL FOR:
HOW AM I SPENDING MY ENERGY?	HOW DO I AFFECT MY WORLD?	
12:00	12:00	
12:30	12:30	
1:00	1:00	
1:30	1:30	
2:00	2:00	SUNDAY
2:30	2:30	INTENTION:
3:00	3:00	
3:30	3:30	
4:00	4:00	MORNING RITUALS AND ACTIVITIES
4:30	4:30	
5:00	5:00	
5:30	5:30	
6:00	6:00	
EVENING RITUALS AND ACTIVITIES	EVENING RITUALS AND ACTIVITIES	
		EVENING RITUALS AND ACTIVITIES
I AM GRATEFUL FOR:	I AM GRATEFUL FOR:	
		I AM GRATEFUL FOR:

DREAM, EXPAND, RECORD, REFLECT:

FOCUS

Rituals for Living Challenge
This week, try neti (nasal irrigation) three times. Use either a neti pot or a cup. Add ¼ to ½ teaspoon salt to 1 cup of warm, clean water make a solution as salty as tears. Pour through the nose. Look online for more details if needed.

TOP 3 GOALS THIS WEEK

TASKS
- MONTHLY PLAN
- INCOMPLETE FROM LAST WEEK
- LIFE DUTIES
- ★ STAR THE MOST IMPORTANT TASKS ★

Final task: schedule next week

NOW: PUT THESE TASKS & RITUALS IN YOUR CALENDAR, GO FORTH AND CONQUER!

MONTH:

	MONDAY	TUESDAY	WEDNESDAY
	INTENTION:	INTENTION:	INTENTION:
	MORNING RITUALS AND ACTIVITIES	MORNING RITUALS AND ACTIVITIES	MORNING RITUALS AND ACTIVITIES
8:00			
8:30			
9:00			
9:30			
10:00			
10:30			
11:00			
11:30			
	WHAT SHALL I BE FOCUSED ON?	WHERE IS MY ATTENTION GOING?	WHAT PERSPECTIVE DO I CHOOSE?
12:00			
12:30			
1:00			
1:30			
2:00			
2:30			
3:00			
3:30			
4:00			
4:30			
5:00			
5:30			
6:00			
	EVENING RITUALS AND ACTIVITIES	EVENING RITUALS AND ACTIVITIES	EVENING RITUALS AND ACTIVITIES
	I AM GRATEFUL FOR:	I AM GRATEFUL FOR:	I AM GRATEFUL FOR:

RITUALS FOR THRIVING

- ○ EXERCISE
- ○ MEDITATE / BREATHE
- ○ JOURNAL
- ○ DANCE
- ○ GO ON A DATE
- ○ CONNECT WITH NATURE
- ○ VISUALIZE
- ○ FAMILY TIME
- ○ COOK / EAT A HEALTHY MEAL
- ○ ORGANIZE MY SPACE / LIFE
- ○ GET RID OF THINGS I DON'T LOVE
- ○ BE WITH FRIENDS
- ○ PLAY
- ○ LET GO / FORGIVE
- ○ SING / MAKE MUSIC
- ○ CREATE ART
- ○ READ FOR ENJOYMENT
- ○ CONNECT / PRAY
- ○ CALL SOMEONE / WRITE A LETTER
- ○ STRETCH / DO YOGA
- ○ MASSAGE / EXCHANGE TOUCH
- ○ SERVE MY COMMUNITY

THURSDAY	FRIDAY	SATURDAY
INTENTION:	INTENTION:	INTENTION:
MORNING RITUALS AND ACTIVITIES	MORNING RITUALS AND ACTIVITIES	MORNING RITUALS AND ACTIVITIES
8:00	8:00	
8:30	8:30	
9:00	9:00	
9:30	9:30	EVENING RITUALS AND ACTIVITIES
10:00	10:00	
10:30	10:30	
11:00	11:00	
11:30	11:30	I AM GRATEFUL FOR:
HOW AM I SPENDING MY ENERGY?	HOW DO I AFFECT MY WORLD?	
12:00	12:00	
12:30	12:30	
1:00	1:00	
1:30	1:30	
2:00	2:00	**SUNDAY**
2:30	2:30	INTENTION:
3:00	3:00	
3:30	3:30	
4:00	4:00	MORNING RITUALS AND ACTIVITIES
4:30	4:30	
5:00	5:00	
5:30	5:30	
6:00	6:00	
EVENING RITUALS AND ACTIVITIES	EVENING RITUALS AND ACTIVITIES	
		EVENING RITUALS AND ACTIVITIES
I AM GRATEFUL FOR:	I AM GRATEFUL FOR:	
		I AM GRATEFUL FOR:

DREAM, EXPAND, RECORD, REFLECT:

Rituals for Living Challenge

This week, find a way to laugh each day. Watch a comedy, have someone tickle you, make faces in the mirror, do something ridiculous, or just start belly laughing loudly until it turns into natural laughter.

TOP 3 GOALS THIS WEEK

TASKS
- MONTHLY PLAN
- INCOMPLETE FROM LAST WEEK
- LIFE DUTIES
- ★ STAR THE MOST IMPORTANT TASKS ★

Final task: schedule next week

NOW: PUT THESE TASKS & RITUALS IN YOUR CALENDAR, GO FORTH AND CONQUER!

MONTH:

	MONDAY	TUESDAY	WEDNESDAY
	INTENTION:	INTENTION:	INTENTION:
	MORNING RITUALS AND ACTIVITIES	MORNING RITUALS AND ACTIVITIES	MORNING RITUALS AND ACTIVITIES
8:00			
8:30			
9:00			
9:30			
10:00			
10:30			
11:00			
11:30			
	WHAT SHALL I BE FOCUSED ON?	WHERE IS MY ATTENTION GOING?	WHAT PERSPECTIVE DO I CHOOSE?
12:00			
12:30			
1:00			
1:30			
2:00			
2:30			
3:00			
3:30			
4:00			
4:30			
5:00			
5:30			
6:00			
	EVENING RITUALS AND ACTIVITIES	EVENING RITUALS AND ACTIVITIES	EVENING RITUALS AND ACTIVITIES
	I AM GRATEFUL FOR:	I AM GRATEFUL FOR:	I AM GRATEFUL FOR:

THURSDAY	FRIDAY	SATURDAY
INTENTION:	INTENTION:	INTENTION:
MORNING RITUALS AND ACTIVITIES	MORNING RITUALS AND ACTIVITIES	MORNING RITUALS AND ACTIVITIES
8:00	8:00	
8:30	8:30	
9:00	9:00	
9:30	9:30	EVENING RITUALS AND ACTIVITIES
10:00	10:00	
10:30	10:30	
11:00	11:00	
11:30	11:30	I AM GRATEFUL FOR:
HOW AM I SPENDING MY ENERGY?	HOW DO I AFFECT MY WORLD?	
12:00	12:00	
12:30	12:30	
1:00	1:00	
1:30	1:30	
2:00	2:00	SUNDAY
2:30	2:30	INTENTION:
3:00	3:00	
3:30	3:30	
4:00	4:00	MORNING RITUALS AND ACTIVITIES
4:30	4:30	
5:00	5:00	
5:30	5:30	
6:00	6:00	
EVENING RITUALS AND ACTIVITIES	EVENING RITUALS AND ACTIVITIES	
		EVENING RITUALS AND ACTIVITIES
I AM GRATEFUL FOR:	I AM GRATEFUL FOR:	
		I AM GRATEFUL FOR:

RITUALS FOR THRIVING

- ○ EXERCISE
- ○ MEDITATE / BREATHE
- ○ JOURNAL
- ○ DANCE
- ○ GO ON A DATE
- ○ CONNECT WITH NATURE
- ○ VISUALIZE
- ○ FAMILY TIME
- ○ COOK / EAT A HEALTHY MEAL
- ○ ORGANIZE MY SPACE / LIFE
- ○ GET RID OF THINGS I DON'T LOVE
- ○ BE WITH FRIENDS
- ○ PLAY
- ○ LET GO / FORGIVE
- ○ SING / MAKE MUSIC
- ○ CREATE ART
- ○ READ FOR ENJOYMENT
- ○ CONNECT / PRAY
- ○ CALL SOMEONE / WRITE A LETTER
- ○ STRETCH / DO YOGA
- ○ MASSAGE / EXCHANGE TOUCH
- ○ SERVE MY COMMUNITY

DREAM, EXPAND, RECORD, REFLECT:

FOCUS

Rituals for Living Challenge
This week, generate as little garbage as possible. Recycle everything you can (try to reduce your recyclables too), compost anything you can, avoid single-use and single-serving packaging, and buy less stuff that will end up in a landfill.

TOP 3 GOALS THIS WEEK

TASKS
- MONTHLY PLAN
- INCOMPLETE FROM LAST WEEK
- LIFE DUTIES
- ★ STAR THE MOST IMPORTANT TASKS ★

Final task: schedule next week
NOW: PUT THESE TASKS & RITUALS IN YOUR CALENDAR, GO FORTH AND CONQUER!

MONTH:

	MONDAY	TUESDAY	WEDNESDAY
	INTENTION:	INTENTION:	INTENTION:
	MORNING RITUALS AND ACTIVITIES	MORNING RITUALS AND ACTIVITIES	MORNING RITUALS AND ACTIVITIES
8:00			
8:30			
9:00			
9:30			
10:00			
10:30			
11:00			
11:30			
	WHAT SHALL I BE FOCUSED ON?	WHERE IS MY ATTENTION GOING?	WHAT PERSPECTIVE DO I CHOOSE?
12:00			
12:30			
1:00			
1:30			
2:00			
2:30			
3:00			
3:30			
4:00			
4:30			
5:00			
5:30			
6:00			
	EVENING RITUALS AND ACTIVITIES	EVENING RITUALS AND ACTIVITIES	EVENING RITUALS AND ACTIVITIES
	I AM GRATEFUL FOR:	I AM GRATEFUL FOR:	I AM GRATEFUL FOR:

THURSDAY	FRIDAY	SATURDAY	RITUALS FOR THRIVING
INTENTION:	INTENTION:	INTENTION:	○ EXERCISE
			○ MEDITATE / BREATHE
			○ JOURNAL
			○ DANCE
			○ GO ON A DATE
MORNING RITUALS AND ACTIVITIES	MORNING RITUALS AND ACTIVITIES	MORNING RITUALS AND ACTIVITIES	○ CONNECT WITH NATURE
			○ VISUALIZE
			○ FAMILY TIME
			○ COOK / EAT A HEALTHY MEAL
			○ ORGANIZE MY SPACE / LIFE
8:00	8:00		○ GET RID OF THINGS I DON'T LOVE
8:30	8:30		○ BE WITH FRIENDS
9:00	9:00		○ PLAY
9:30	9:30	EVENING RITUALS AND ACTIVITIES	○ LET GO / FORGIVE
10:00	10:00		○ SING / MAKE MUSIC
10:30	10:30		○ CREATE ART
11:00	11:00		○ READ FOR ENJOYMENT
11:30	11:30	I AM GRATEFUL FOR:	○ CONNECT / PRAY
HOW AM I SPENDING MY ENERGY?	HOW DO I AFFECT MY WORLD?		○ CALL SOMEONE / WRITE A LETTER
12:00	12:00		○ STRETCH / DO YOGA
12:30	12:30		○ MASSAGE / EXCHANGE TOUCH
1:00	1:00		○ SERVE MY COMMUNITY
1:30	1:30		
2:00	2:00	SUNDAY	DREAM, EXPAND, RECORD, REFLECT:
2:30	2:30	INTENTION:	
3:00	3:00		
3:30	3:30		
4:00	4:00	MORNING RITUALS AND ACTIVITIES	
4:30	4:30		
5:00	5:00		
5:30	5:30		
6:00	6:00		
EVENING RITUALS AND ACTIVITIES	EVENING RITUALS AND ACTIVITIES		
		EVENING RITUALS AND ACTIVITIES	
I AM GRATEFUL FOR:	I AM GRATEFUL FOR:		
		I AM GRATEFUL FOR:	

Rituals for Living Challenge

Optimize bowel health this week. Have plenty of water, lots of fiber (veggies, fruits, beans, oats), good fats (olive oil, flax, avocado, hemp, chia, etc.), exercise your abdomen, eat cultured foods, de-stress, and try squatting when you go.

TOP 3 GOALS THIS WEEK

TASKS
- MONTHLY PLAN
- INCOMPLETE FROM LAST WEEK
- LIFE DUTIES
- ★ STAR THE MOST IMPORTANT TASKS ★

Final task: schedule next week

NOW: PUT THESE TASKS & RITUALS IN YOUR CALENDAR, GO FORTH AND CONQUER!

MONTH:

	MONDAY	TUESDAY	WEDNESDAY
	INTENTION:	INTENTION:	INTENTION:
	MORNING RITUALS AND ACTIVITIES	MORNING RITUALS AND ACTIVITIES	MORNING RITUALS AND ACTIVITIES
8:00			
8:30			
9:00			
9:30			
10:00			
10:30			
11:00			
11:30			
	WHAT SHALL I BE FOCUSED ON?	WHERE IS MY ATTENTION GOING?	WHAT PERSPECTIVE DO I CHOOSE?
12:00			
12:30			
1:00			
1:30			
2:00			
2:30			
3:00			
3:30			
4:00			
4:30			
5:00			
5:30			
6:00			
	EVENING RITUALS AND ACTIVITIES	EVENING RITUALS AND ACTIVITIES	EVENING RITUALS AND ACTIVITIES
	I AM GRATEFUL FOR:	I AM GRATEFUL FOR:	I AM GRATEFUL FOR:

RITUALS FOR THRIVING

- ○ EXERCISE
- ○ MEDITATE / BREATHE
- ○ JOURNAL
- ○ DANCE
- ○ GO ON A DATE
- ○ CONNECT WITH NATURE
- ○ VISUALIZE
- ○ FAMILY TIME
- ○ COOK / EAT A HEALTHY MEAL
- ○ ORGANIZE MY SPACE / LIFE
- ○ GET RID OF THINGS I DON'T LOVE
- ○ BE WITH FRIENDS
- ○ PLAY
- ○ LET GO / FORGIVE
- ○ SING / MAKE MUSIC
- ○ CREATE ART
- ○ READ FOR ENJOYMENT
- ○ CONNECT / PRAY
- ○ CALL SOMEONE / WRITE A LETTER
- ○ STRETCH / DO YOGA
- ○ MASSAGE / EXCHANGE TOUCH
- ○ SERVE MY COMMUNITY

THURSDAY	FRIDAY	SATURDAY
INTENTION:	INTENTION:	INTENTION:
MORNING RITUALS AND ACTIVITIES	MORNING RITUALS AND ACTIVITIES	MORNING RITUALS AND ACTIVITIES
8:00	8:00	
8:30	8:30	
9:00	9:00	
9:30	9:30	EVENING RITUALS AND ACTIVITIES
10:00	10:00	
10:30	10:30	
11:00	11:00	
11:30	11:30	I AM GRATEFUL FOR:
HOW AM I SPENDING MY ENERGY?	HOW DO I AFFECT MY WORLD?	
12:00	12:00	
12:30	12:30	
1:00	1:00	
1:30	1:30	
2:00	2:00	SUNDAY
2:30	2:30	INTENTION:
3:00	3:00	
3:30	3:30	
4:00	4:00	MORNING RITUALS AND ACTIVITIES
4:30	4:30	
5:00	5:00	
5:30	5:30	
6:00	6:00	
EVENING RITUALS AND ACTIVITIES	EVENING RITUALS AND ACTIVITIES	
		EVENING RITUALS AND ACTIVITIES
I AM GRATEFUL FOR:	I AM GRATEFUL FOR:	
		I AM GRATEFUL FOR:

DREAM, EXPAND, RECORD, REFLECT:

Rituals for Living Challenge

This week, turn up the volume on your inner pessimist. Don't let negative thoughts run you from 'below the radar.' Make the thoughts "loud" enough to hear them, hen challenge them, laugh at them, breathe into them, forgive them.

TOP 3 GOALS THIS WEEK

TASKS
- MONTHLY PLAN
- INCOMPLETE FROM LAST WEEK
- LIFE DUTIES
- ★ STAR THE MOST IMPORTANT TASKS ★

Final task: schedule next week

NOW: PUT THESE TASKS & RITUALS IN YOUR CALENDAR, GO FORTH AND CONQUER!

MONTH:

	MONDAY	TUESDAY	WEDNESDAY
	INTENTION:	**INTENTION:**	**INTENTION:**
	MORNING RITUALS AND ACTIVITIES	**MORNING RITUALS AND ACTIVITIES**	**MORNING RITUALS AND ACTIVITIES**
8:00			
8:30			
9:00			
9:30			
10:00			
10:30			
11:00			
11:30			
	WHAT SHALL I BE FOCUSED ON?	**WHERE IS MY ATTENTION GOING?**	**WHAT PERSPECTIVE DO I CHOOSE?**
12:00			
12:30			
1:00			
1:30			
2:00			
2:30			
3:00			
3:30			
4:00			
4:30			
5:00			
5:30			
6:00			
	EVENING RITUALS AND ACTIVITIES	**EVENING RITUALS AND ACTIVITIES**	**EVENING RITUALS AND ACTIVITIES**
	I AM GRATEFUL FOR:	**I AM GRATEFUL FOR:**	**I AM GRATEFUL FOR:**

RITUALS FOR THRIVING

- ○ EXERCISE
- ○ MEDITATE / BREATHE
- ○ JOURNAL
- ○ DANCE
- ○ GO ON A DATE
- ○ CONNECT WITH NATURE
- ○ VISUALIZE
- ○ FAMILY TIME
- ○ COOK / EAT A HEALTHY MEAL
- ○ ORGANIZE MY SPACE / LIFE
- ○ GET RID OF THINGS I DON'T LOVE
- ○ BE WITH FRIENDS
- ○ PLAY
- ○ LET GO / FORGIVE
- ○ SING / MAKE MUSIC
- ○ CREATE ART
- ○ READ FOR ENJOYMENT
- ○ CONNECT / PRAY
- ○ CALL SOMEONE / WRITE A LETTER
- ○ STRETCH / DO YOGA
- ○ MASSAGE / EXCHANGE TOUCH
- ○ SERVE MY COMMUNITY

THURSDAY	FRIDAY	SATURDAY
INTENTION:	INTENTION:	INTENTION:
MORNING RITUALS AND ACTIVITIES	MORNING RITUALS AND ACTIVITIES	MORNING RITUALS AND ACTIVITIES
8:00	8:00	
8:30	8:30	
9:00	9:00	
9:30	9:30	EVENING RITUALS AND ACTIVITIES
10:00	10:00	
10:30	10:30	
11:00	11:00	
11:30	11:30	I AM GRATEFUL FOR:
HOW AM I SPENDING MY ENERGY?	HOW DO I AFFECT MY WORLD?	
12:00	12:00	
12:30	12:30	
1:00	1:00	
1:30	1:30	
2:00	2:00	SUNDAY
2:30	2:30	INTENTION:
3:00	3:00	
3:30	3:30	
4:00	4:00	MORNING RITUALS AND ACTIVITIES
4:30	4:30	
5:00	5:00	
5:30	5:30	
6:00	6:00	
EVENING RITUALS AND ACTIVITIES	EVENING RITUALS AND ACTIVITIES	
		EVENING RITUALS AND ACTIVITIES
I AM GRATEFUL FOR:	I AM GRATEFUL FOR:	
		I AM GRATEFUL FOR:

DREAM, EXPAND, RECORD, REFLECT:

FOCUS

Rituals for Living Challenge
Look and listen for good signs, beauty, & fascinating things. Talk about them, share them, amplify them, savor them. Imagine you tapped into a vein of gold, and now follow it. Jump from one good thing to the next. Make a game of it.

TOP 3 GOALS THIS WEEK

TASKS
- MONTHLY PLAN
- INCOMPLETE FROM LAST WEEK
- LIFE DUTIES
- ★ STAR THE MOST IMPORTANT TASKS ★

Final task: schedule next week

NOW: PUT THESE TASKS & RITUALS IN YOUR CALENDAR, GO FORTH AND CONQUER!

MONTH:

	MONDAY	TUESDAY	WEDNESDAY
	INTENTION:	INTENTION:	INTENTION:
	MORNING RITUALS AND ACTIVITIES	MORNING RITUALS AND ACTIVITIES	MORNING RITUALS AND ACTIVITIES
8:00			
8:30			
9:00			
9:30			
10:00			
10:30			
11:00			
11:30			
	WHAT SHALL I BE FOCUSED ON?	WHERE IS MY ATTENTION GOING?	WHAT PERSPECTIVE DO I CHOOSE?
12:00			
12:30			
1:00			
1:30			
2:00			
2:30			
3:00			
3:30			
4:00			
4:30			
5:00			
5:30			
6:00			
	EVENING RITUALS AND ACTIVITIES	EVENING RITUALS AND ACTIVITIES	EVENING RITUALS AND ACTIVITIES
	I AM GRATEFUL FOR:	I AM GRATEFUL FOR:	I AM GRATEFUL FOR:

RITUALS FOR THRIVING

- ○ EXERCISE
- ○ MEDITATE / BREATHE
- ○ JOURNAL
- ○ DANCE
- ○ GO ON A DATE
- ○ CONNECT WITH NATURE
- ○ VISUALIZE
- ○ FAMILY TIME
- ○ COOK / EAT A HEALTHY MEAL
- ○ ORGANIZE MY SPACE / LIFE
- ○ GET RID OF THINGS I DON'T LOVE
- ○ BE WITH FRIENDS
- ○ PLAY
- ○ LET GO / FORGIVE
- ○ SING / MAKE MUSIC
- ○ CREATE ART
- ○ READ FOR ENJOYMENT
- ○ CONNECT / PRAY
- ○ CALL SOMEONE / WRITE A LETTER
- ○ STRETCH / DO YOGA
- ○ MASSAGE / EXCHANGE TOUCH
- ○ SERVE MY COMMUNITY

THURSDAY	FRIDAY	SATURDAY
INTENTION:	INTENTION:	INTENTION:
MORNING RITUALS AND ACTIVITIES	MORNING RITUALS AND ACTIVITIES	MORNING RITUALS AND ACTIVITIES
8:00	8:00	
8:30	8:30	
9:00	9:00	
9:30	9:30	EVENING RITUALS AND ACTIVITIES
10:00	10:00	
10:30	10:30	
11:00	11:00	
11:30	11:30	I AM GRATEFUL FOR:
HOW AM I SPENDING MY ENERGY?	HOW DO I AFFECT MY WORLD?	
12:00	12:00	
12:30	12:30	
1:00	1:00	
1:30	1:30	
2:00	2:00	**SUNDAY**
2:30	2:30	INTENTION:
3:00	3:00	
3:30	3:30	
4:00	4:00	MORNING RITUALS AND ACTIVITIES
4:30	4:30	
5:00	5:00	
5:30	5:30	
6:00	6:00	
EVENING RITUALS AND ACTIVITIES	EVENING RITUALS AND ACTIVITIES	
		EVENING RITUALS AND ACTIVITIES
I AM GRATEFUL FOR:	I AM GRATEFUL FOR:	
		I AM GRATEFUL FOR:

DREAM, EXPAND, RECORD, REFLECT:

FOCUS

Rituals for Living Challenge
This week, take a break from stimulants – coffee, caffeinated tea, yerba mate, etc. Ideally sugar, too. Don't let them rob your energy stores or mask your true energy level (and keep you from addressing the cause, if it's low).

TOP 3 GOALS THIS WEEK

TASKS
- MONTHLY PLAN
- INCOMPLETE FROM LAST WEEK
- LIFE DUTIES
- ★ STAR THE MOST IMPORTANT TASKS ★

Final task: schedule next week

NOW: PUT THESE TASKS & RITUALS IN YOUR CALENDAR, GO FORTH AND CONQUER!

MONTH:

	MONDAY	TUESDAY	WEDNESDAY
	INTENTION:	INTENTION:	INTENTION:
	MORNING RITUALS AND ACTIVITIES	MORNING RITUALS AND ACTIVITIES	MORNING RITUALS AND ACTIVITIES
8:00			
8:30			
9:00			
9:30			
10:00			
10:30			
11:00			
11:30			
	WHAT SHALL I BE FOCUSED ON?	WHERE IS MY ATTENTION GOING?	WHAT PERSPECTIVE DO I CHOOSE?
12:00			
12:30			
1:00			
1:30			
2:00			
2:30			
3:00			
3:30			
4:00			
4:30			
5:00			
5:30			
6:00			
	EVENING RITUALS AND ACTIVITIES	EVENING RITUALS AND ACTIVITIES	EVENING RITUALS AND ACTIVITIES
	I AM GRATEFUL FOR:	I AM GRATEFUL FOR:	I AM GRATEFUL FOR:

RITUALS FOR THRIVING

- ○ EXERCISE
- ○ MEDITATE / BREATHE
- ○ JOURNAL
- ○ DANCE
- ○ GO ON A DATE
- ○ CONNECT WITH NATURE
- ○ VISUALIZE
- ○ FAMILY TIME
- ○ COOK / EAT A HEALTHY MEAL
- ○ ORGANIZE MY SPACE / LIFE
- ○ GET RID OF THINGS I DON'T LOVE
- ○ BE WITH FRIENDS
- ○ PLAY
- ○ LET GO / FORGIVE
- ○ SING / MAKE MUSIC
- ○ CREATE ART
- ○ READ FOR ENJOYMENT
- ○ CONNECT / PRAY
- ○ CALL SOMEONE / WRITE A LETTER
- ○ STRETCH / DO YOGA
- ○ MASSAGE / EXCHANGE TOUCH
- ○ SERVE MY COMMUNITY

THURSDAY	FRIDAY	SATURDAY
INTENTION:	INTENTION:	INTENTION:
MORNING RITUALS AND ACTIVITIES	MORNING RITUALS AND ACTIVITIES	MORNING RITUALS AND ACTIVITIES
8:00	8:00	
8:30	8:30	
9:00	9:00	
9:30	9:30	EVENING RITUALS AND ACTIVITIES
10:00	10:00	
10:30	10:30	
11:00	11:00	
11:30	11:30	I AM GRATEFUL FOR:
HOW AM I SPENDING MY ENERGY?	HOW DO I AFFECT MY WORLD?	
12:00	12:00	
12:30	12:30	
1:00	1:00	
1:30	1:30	
2:00	2:00	SUNDAY
2:30	2:30	INTENTION:
3:00	3:00	
3:30	3:30	
4:00	4:00	MORNING RITUALS AND ACTIVITIES
4:30	4:30	
5:00	5:00	
5:30	5:30	
6:00	6:00	
EVENING RITUALS AND ACTIVITIES	EVENING RITUALS AND ACTIVITIES	
		EVENING RITUALS AND ACTIVITIES
I AM GRATEFUL FOR:	I AM GRATEFUL FOR:	
		I AM GRATEFUL FOR:

DREAM, EXPAND, RECORD, REFLECT:

Rituals for Living Challenge

This week, pretend you are an enlightened being. A sage. Embody this fully. How does your patience change? How is your perspective different? How do you treat others differently? How do you respond to having your buttons pushed?

TOP 3 GOALS THIS WEEK

TASKS
- **MONTHLY PLAN**
- **INCOMPLETE FROM LAST WEEK**
- **LIFE DUTIES**
- ★ **STAR THE MOST IMPORTANT TASKS** ★

Final task: schedule next week

NOW: PUT THESE TASKS & RITUALS IN YOUR CALENDAR, GO FORTH AND CONQUER!

MONTH:

	MONDAY	TUESDAY	WEDNESDAY
	INTENTION:	**INTENTION:**	**INTENTION:**
	MORNING RITUALS AND ACTIVITIES	**MORNING RITUALS AND ACTIVITIES**	**MORNING RITUALS AND ACTIVITIES**
8:00			
8:30			
9:00			
9:30			
10:00			
10:30			
11:00			
11:30			
	WHAT SHALL I BE FOCUSED ON?	**WHERE IS MY ATTENTION GOING?**	**WHAT PERSPECTIVE DO I CHOOSE?**
12:00			
12:30			
1:00			
1:30			
2:00			
2:30			
3:00			
3:30			
4:00			
4:30			
5:00			
5:30			
6:00			
	EVENING RITUALS AND ACTIVITIES	**EVENING RITUALS AND ACTIVITIES**	**EVENING RITUALS AND ACTIVITIES**
	I AM GRATEFUL FOR:	**I AM GRATEFUL FOR:**	**I AM GRATEFUL FOR:**

THURSDAY	FRIDAY	SATURDAY
INTENTION:	INTENTION:	INTENTION:
MORNING RITUALS AND ACTIVITIES	MORNING RITUALS AND ACTIVITIES	MORNING RITUALS AND ACTIVITIES
8:00	8:00	
8:30	8:30	
9:00	9:00	
9:30	9:30	EVENING RITUALS AND ACTIVITIES
10:00	10:00	
10:30	10:30	
11:00	11:00	
11:30	11:30	I AM GRATEFUL FOR:
HOW AM I SPENDING MY ENERGY?	HOW DO I AFFECT MY WORLD?	
12:00	12:00	
12:30	12:30	
1:00	1:00	
1:30	1:30	
2:00	2:00	SUNDAY
2:30	2:30	INTENTION:
3:00	3:00	
3:30	3:30	
4:00	4:00	MORNING RITUALS AND ACTIVITIES
4:30	4:30	
5:00	5:00	
5:30	5:30	
6:00	6:00	
EVENING RITUALS AND ACTIVITIES	EVENING RITUALS AND ACTIVITIES	
		EVENING RITUALS AND ACTIVITIES
I AM GRATEFUL FOR:	I AM GRATEFUL FOR:	
		I AM GRATEFUL FOR:

RITUALS FOR THRIVING

- ○ EXERCISE
- ○ MEDITATE / BREATHE
- ○ JOURNAL
- ○ DANCE
- ○ GO ON A DATE
- ○ CONNECT WITH NATURE
- ○ VISUALIZE
- ○ FAMILY TIME
- ○ COOK / EAT A HEALTHY MEAL
- ○ ORGANIZE MY SPACE / LIFE
- ○ GET RID OF THINGS I DON'T LOVE
- ○ BE WITH FRIENDS
- ○ PLAY
- ○ LET GO / FORGIVE
- ○ SING / MAKE MUSIC
- ○ CREATE ART
- ○ READ FOR ENJOYMENT
- ○ CONNECT / PRAY
- ○ CALL SOMEONE / WRITE A LETTER
- ○ STRETCH / DO YOGA
- ○ MASSAGE / EXCHANGE TOUCH
- ○ SERVE MY COMMUNITY

DREAM, EXPAND, RECORD, REFLECT:

It's time to reflect on the past quarter and decide what you want to refine as you move forward.

1. What was your biggest time and/or energy waster in the past quarter?

_____

_____

2. Which activities and rituals yielded the biggest "return" for you (either tangible or intangible) in the past quarter?

_____

_____

3. Is there anything you've been procrastinating over the past quarter?

_____

_____

4. Which of the items from the Rituals for Thriving list did you never do but would like to?

_____

_____

5. If anything happened in the last quarter that you would like to *reframe* (i.e., change the story you tell yourself and others about it, so as to hold it in a more positive light), please explain how you intend to reframe it.

_____

_____

_____

6. What has been infringing on your happiness, health, or productivity in the past quarter that you intend to let go of in the coming quarter?

_____

_____

_____

NOW, use these answers to shape your focus and refine your thoughts and behaviors in the coming quarter!

Quarter Four Breakdown

1. Get into your *ritual for planning* space. Do whatever you do to tune in (light a candle, take a breath, go to a peaceful spot, set an intention, etc.).

2 Look back at your What I Will Accomplish This Year list, and find all the projects that will be occurring in the coming quarter. Write each one in the table below and mark the appropriate month number(s) for the month(s) in which it will taking place. There is space at the top of the Month column to write abbreviations of the names of the months above ① ② and ③.

Project	Month		
	①	②	③
	①	②	③
	①	②	③
	①	②	③
	①	②	③
	①	②	③
	①	②	③
	①	②	③
	①	②	③
	①	②	③
	①	②	③
	①	②	③
	①	②	③
	①	②	③
	①	②	③
	①	②	③
	①	②	③
	①	②	③
	①	②	③
	①	②	③
	①	②	③
	①	②	③
	①	②	③

Month:

1. Get into your *ritual for planning* space.

2. Gather the projects from the Quarterly Breakdown that pertain to this month and write each one on a PROJECT line below.

3. Under the project name, enter all of the tasks that are involved in the project. Each of these tasks must be a single action step, so that it can be put into your calendar and when you see it, no analysis needs to occur – you know exactly what to do.

PROJECT

_____ _____
_____ _____
_____ _____
_____ _____
_____ _____
_____ _____
_____ _____

PROJECT

_____ _____
_____ _____
_____ _____
_____ _____
_____ _____
_____ _____
_____ _____

PROJECT

PROJECT

PROJECT

MONTH:

Monday	Tuesday	Wednesday

Notes:

Thursday	Friday	Saturday	Sunday

Month:

1. Get into your *ritual for planning* space.

2. Gather the projects from the Quarterly Breakdown that pertain to this month and write each one on a PROJECT line below.

3. Under the project name, enter all of the tasks that are involved in the project. Each of these tasks must be a single action step, so that it can be put into your calendar and when you see it, no analysis needs to occur – you know exactly what to do.

PROJECT

PROJECT

PROJECT

PROJECT

PROJECT

MONTH:

Monday	Tuesday	Wednesday

Notes:

Thursday	Friday	Saturday	Sunday

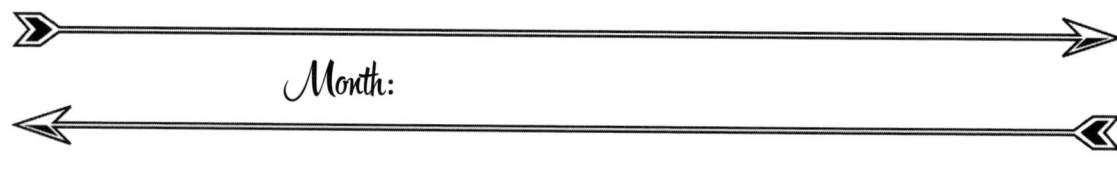

Month:

1. Get into your *ritual for planning* space.

2. Gather the projects from the Quarterly Breakdown that pertain to this month and write each one on a PROJECT line below.

3. Under the project name, enter all of the tasks that are involved in the project. Each of these tasks must be a single action step, so that it can be put into your calendar and when you see it, no analysis needs to occur – you know exactly what to do.

_____
PROJECT

_____ _____
_____ _____
_____ _____
_____ _____
_____ _____
_____ _____
_____ _____

_____
PROJECT

_____ _____
_____ _____
_____ _____
_____ _____
_____ _____
_____ _____
_____ _____

PROJECT

PROJECT

PROJECT

MONTH:

Monday	Tuesday	Wednesday

Notes:

Thursday	Friday	Saturday	Sunday

Rituals for Living Challenge

3 times this week, be a solar panel. Stand in the sun (if it's always behind clouds, that's ok). Face your palms toward it at chest level. Imagine you're absorbing solar energy through your palms, storing it in your body, charging your batteries.

TOP 3 GOALS THIS WEEK

TASKS
- MONTHLY PLAN
- INCOMPLETE FROM LAST WEEK
- LIFE DUTIES
- ★ STAR THE MOST IMPORTANT TASKS ★

Final task: schedule next week

NOW: PUT THESE TASKS & RITUALS IN YOUR CALENDAR, GO FORTH AND CONQUER!

MONTH:

	MONDAY	TUESDAY	WEDNESDAY
	INTENTION:	INTENTION:	INTENTION:
	MORNING RITUALS AND ACTIVITIES	MORNING RITUALS AND ACTIVITIES	MORNING RITUALS AND ACTIVITIES
8:00			
8:30			
9:00			
9:30			
10:00			
10:30			
11:00			
11:30			
	WHAT SHALL I BE FOCUSED ON?	WHERE IS MY ATTENTION GOING?	WHAT PERSPECTIVE DO I CHOOSE?
12:00			
12:30			
1:00			
1:30			
2:00			
2:30			
3:00			
3:30			
4:00			
4:30			
5:00			
5:30			
6:00			
	EVENING RITUALS AND ACTIVITIES	EVENING RITUALS AND ACTIVITIES	EVENING RITUALS AND ACTIVITIES
	I AM GRATEFUL FOR:	I AM GRATEFUL FOR:	I AM GRATEFUL FOR:

THURSDAY	FRIDAY	SATURDAY	RITUALS FOR THRIVING
INTENTION:	INTENTION:	INTENTION:	○ EXERCISE
			○ MEDITATE / BREATHE
			○ JOURNAL
			○ DANCE
			○ GO ON A DATE
MORNING RITUALS AND ACTIVITIES	MORNING RITUALS AND ACTIVITIES	MORNING RITUALS AND ACTIVITIES	○ CONNECT WITH NATURE
			○ VISUALIZE
			○ FAMILY TIME
			○ COOK / EAT A HEALTHY MEAL
			○ ORGANIZE MY SPACE / LIFE
8:00	8:00		○ GET RID OF THINGS I DON'T LOVE
8:30	8:30		○ BE WITH FRIENDS
9:00	9:00		○ PLAY
9:30	9:30	EVENING RITUALS AND ACTIVITIES	○ LET GO / FORGIVE
10:00	10:00		○ SING / MAKE MUSIC
10:30	10:30		○ CREATE ART
11:00	11:00		○ READ FOR ENJOYMENT
11:30	11:30	I AM GRATEFUL FOR:	○ CONNECT / PRAY
HOW AM I SPENDING MY ENERGY?	HOW DO I AFFECT MY WORLD?		○ CALL SOMEONE / WRITE A LETTER
12:00	12:00		○ STRETCH / DO YOGA
12:30	12:30		○ MASSAGE / EXCHANGE TOUCH
1:00	1:00		○ SERVE MY COMMUNITY
1:30	1:30		
2:00	2:00	SUNDAY	DREAM, EXPAND, RECORD, REFLECT:
2:30	2:30	INTENTION:	
3:00	3:00		
3:30	3:30		
4:00	4:00	MORNING RITUALS AND ACTIVITIES	
4:30	4:30		
5:00	5:00		
5:30	5:30		
6:00	6:00		
EVENING RITUALS AND ACTIVITIES	EVENING RITUALS AND ACTIVITIES		
		EVENING RITUALS AND ACTIVITIES	
I AM GRATEFUL FOR:	I AM GRATEFUL FOR:		
		I AM GRATEFUL FOR:	

FOCUS

Rituals for Living Challenge

This week, connect your whole body in all your movements. When you stand up, sit down, walk around, wash dishes, take a shower, etc., engage every muscle and joint, including your abdomen & back. Be graceful. Dance through your day.

TOP 3 GOALS THIS WEEK

TASKS
- MONTHLY PLAN
- INCOMPLETE FROM LAST WEEK
- LIFE DUTIES
- ★ STAR THE MOST IMPORTANT TASKS ★

Final task: schedule next week

NOW: PUT THESE TASKS & RITUALS IN YOUR CALENDAR, GO FORTH AND CONQUER!

MONTH:

	MONDAY	TUESDAY	WEDNESDAY
	INTENTION:	INTENTION:	INTENTION:
	MORNING RITUALS AND ACTIVITIES	MORNING RITUALS AND ACTIVITIES	MORNING RITUALS AND ACTIVITIES
8:00			
8:30			
9:00			
9:30			
10:00			
10:30			
11:00			
11:30			
	WHAT SHALL I BE FOCUSED ON?	WHERE IS MY ATTENTION GOING?	WHAT PERSPECTIVE DO I CHOOSE?
12:00			
12:30			
1:00			
1:30			
2:00			
2:30			
3:00			
3:30			
4:00			
4:30			
5:00			
5:30			
6:00			
	EVENING RITUALS AND ACTIVITIES	EVENING RITUALS AND ACTIVITIES	EVENING RITUALS AND ACTIVITIES
	I AM GRATEFUL FOR:	I AM GRATEFUL FOR:	I AM GRATEFUL FOR:

RITUALS FOR THRIVING

- ○ EXERCISE
- ○ MEDITATE / BREATHE
- ○ JOURNAL
- ○ DANCE
- ○ GO ON A DATE
- ○ CONNECT WITH NATURE
- ○ VISUALIZE
- ○ FAMILY TIME
- ○ COOK / EAT A HEALTHY MEAL
- ○ ORGANIZE MY SPACE / LIFE
- ○ GET RID OF THINGS I DON'T LOVE
- ○ BE WITH FRIENDS
- ○ PLAY
- ○ LET GO / FORGIVE
- ○ SING / MAKE MUSIC
- ○ CREATE ART
- ○ READ FOR ENJOYMENT
- ○ CONNECT / PRAY
- ○ CALL SOMEONE / WRITE A LETTER
- ○ STRETCH / DO YOGA
- ○ MASSAGE / EXCHANGE TOUCH
- ○ SERVE MY COMMUNITY

THURSDAY	FRIDAY	SATURDAY
INTENTION:	INTENTION:	INTENTION:
MORNING RITUALS AND ACTIVITIES	MORNING RITUALS AND ACTIVITIES	MORNING RITUALS AND ACTIVITIES
8:00	8:00	
8:30	8:30	
9:00	9:00	
9:30	9:30	EVENING RITUALS AND ACTIVITIES
10:00	10:00	
10:30	10:30	
11:00	11:00	
11:30	11:30	I AM GRATEFUL FOR:
HOW AM I SPENDING MY ENERGY?	HOW DO I AFFECT MY WORLD?	
12:00	12:00	
12:30	12:30	
1:00	1:00	
1:30	1:30	
2:00	2:00	SUNDAY
2:30	2:30	INTENTION:
3:00	3:00	
3:30	3:30	
4:00	4:00	MORNING RITUALS AND ACTIVITIES
4:30	4:30	
5:00	5:00	
5:30	5:30	
6:00	6:00	
EVENING RITUALS AND ACTIVITIES	EVENING RITUALS AND ACTIVITIES	
		EVENING RITUALS AND ACTIVITIES
I AM GRATEFUL FOR:	I AM GRATEFUL FOR:	
		I AM GRATEFUL FOR:

DREAM, EXPAND, RECORD, REFLECT:

FOCUS

Rituals for Living Challenge
This week, be an emissary of love. Imagine you have love beaming out of your heart, your eyes, & your voice, and that it's your mission to share it with the world. Every interaction – with people, animals, and nature – is an opportunity.

TOP 3 GOALS THIS WEEK

TASKS
- MONTHLY PLAN
- INCOMPLETE FROM LAST WEEK
- LIFE DUTIES
- ★ STAR THE MOST IMPORTANT TASKS ★

Final task: schedule next week

NOW: PUT THESE TASKS & RITUALS IN YOUR CALENDAR, GO FORTH AND CONQUER!

MONTH:

	MONDAY	TUESDAY	WEDNESDAY
	INTENTION:	INTENTION:	INTENTION:
	MORNING RITUALS AND ACTIVITIES	MORNING RITUALS AND ACTIVITIES	MORNING RITUALS AND ACTIVITIES
8:00			
8:30			
9:00			
9:30			
10:00			
10:30			
11:00			
11:30			
	WHAT SHALL I BE FOCUSED ON?	WHERE IS MY ATTENTION GOING?	WHAT PERSPECTIVE DO I CHOOSE?
12:00			
12:30			
1:00			
1:30			
2:00			
2:30			
3:00			
3:30			
4:00			
4:30			
5:00			
5:30			
6:00			
	EVENING RITUALS AND ACTIVITIES	EVENING RITUALS AND ACTIVITIES	EVENING RITUALS AND ACTIVITIES
	I AM GRATEFUL FOR:	I AM GRATEFUL FOR:	I AM GRATEFUL FOR:

THURSDAY	FRIDAY	SATURDAY
INTENTION:	INTENTION:	INTENTION:
MORNING RITUALS AND ACTIVITIES	MORNING RITUALS AND ACTIVITIES	MORNING RITUALS AND ACTIVITIES
8:00	8:00	
8:30	8:30	
9:00	9:00	
9:30	9:30	EVENING RITUALS AND ACTIVITIES
10:00	10:00	
10:30	10:30	
11:00	11:00	
11:30	11:30	I AM GRATEFUL FOR:
HOW AM I SPENDING MY ENERGY?	HOW DO I AFFECT MY WORLD?	
12:00	12:00	
12:30	12:30	
1:00	1:00	
1:30	1:30	
2:00	2:00	SUNDAY
2:30	2:30	INTENTION:
3:00	3:00	
3:30	3:30	
4:00	4:00	MORNING RITUALS AND ACTIVITIES
4:30	4:30	
5:00	5:00	
5:30	5:30	
6:00	6:00	
EVENING RITUALS AND ACTIVITIES	EVENING RITUALS AND ACTIVITIES	
		EVENING RITUALS AND ACTIVITIES
I AM GRATEFUL FOR:	I AM GRATEFUL FOR:	
		I AM GRATEFUL FOR:

RITUALS FOR THRIVING

- ◯ EXERCISE
- ◯ MEDITATE / BREATHE
- ◯ JOURNAL
- ◯ DANCE
- ◯ GO ON A DATE
- ◯ CONNECT WITH NATURE
- ◯ VISUALIZE
- ◯ FAMILY TIME
- ◯ COOK / EAT A HEALTHY MEAL
- ◯ ORGANIZE MY SPACE / LIFE
- ◯ GET RID OF THINGS I DON'T LOVE
- ◯ BE WITH FRIENDS
- ◯ PLAY
- ◯ LET GO / FORGIVE
- ◯ SING / MAKE MUSIC
- ◯ CREATE ART
- ◯ READ FOR ENJOYMENT
- ◯ CONNECT / PRAY
- ◯ CALL SOMEONE / WRITE A LETTER
- ◯ STRETCH / DO YOGA
- ◯ MASSAGE / EXCHANGE TOUCH
- ◯ SERVE MY COMMUNITY

DREAM, EXPAND, RECORD, REFLECT:

FOCUS

Rituals for Living Challenge
This week, eat slowly. Chew thoroughly. Put your food / fork down after every bite. Don't put anything into your mouth until you have swallowed the last bite.
Breathe. Savor.
Stop eating before you feel **full**.

TOP 3 GOALS THIS WEEK

TASKS
- MONTHLY PLAN
- INCOMPLETE FROM LAST WEEK
- LIFE DUTIES
- ★ STAR THE MOST IMPORTANT TASKS ★

Final task: schedule next week
NOW: PUT THESE TASKS & RITUALS IN YOUR CALENDAR, GO FORTH AND CONQUER!

MONTH:

	MONDAY	TUESDAY	WEDNESDAY
	INTENTION:	INTENTION:	INTENTION:
	MORNING RITUALS AND ACTIVITIES	MORNING RITUALS AND ACTIVITIES	MORNING RITUALS AND ACTIVITIES
8:00			
8:30			
9:00			
9:30			
10:00			
10:30			
11:00			
11:30			
	WHAT SHALL I BE FOCUSED ON?	WHERE IS MY ATTENTION GOING?	WHAT PERSPECTIVE DO I CHOOSE?
12:00			
12:30			
1:00			
1:30			
2:00			
2:30			
3:00			
3:30			
4:00			
4:30			
5:00			
5:30			
6:00			
	EVENING RITUALS AND ACTIVITIES	EVENING RITUALS AND ACTIVITIES	EVENING RITUALS AND ACTIVITIES
	I AM GRATEFUL FOR:	I AM GRATEFUL FOR:	I AM GRATEFUL FOR:

THURSDAY	FRIDAY	SATURDAY
INTENTION:	INTENTION:	INTENTION:
MORNING RITUALS AND ACTIVITIES	MORNING RITUALS AND ACTIVITIES	MORNING RITUALS AND ACTIVITIES
8:00	8:00	
8:30	8:30	
9:00	9:00	
9:30	9:30	EVENING RITUALS AND ACTIVITIES
10:00	10:00	
10:30	10:30	
11:00	11:00	
11:30	11:30	I AM GRATEFUL FOR:
HOW AM I SPENDING MY ENERGY?	HOW DO I AFFECT MY WORLD?	
12:00	12:00	
12:30	12:30	
1:00	1:00	
1:30	1:30	
2:00	2:00	SUNDAY
2:30	2:30	INTENTION:
3:00	3:00	
3:30	3:30	
4:00	4:00	MORNING RITUALS AND ACTIVITIES
4:30	4:30	
5:00	5:00	
5:30	5:30	
6:00	6:00	
EVENING RITUALS AND ACTIVITIES	EVENING RITUALS AND ACTIVITIES	
		EVENING RITUALS AND ACTIVITIES
I AM GRATEFUL FOR:	I AM GRATEFUL FOR:	
		I AM GRATEFUL FOR:

RITUALS FOR THRIVING

- ○ EXERCISE
- ○ MEDITATE / BREATHE
- ○ JOURNAL
- ○ DANCE
- ○ GO ON A DATE
- ○ CONNECT WITH NATURE
- ○ VISUALIZE
- ○ FAMILY TIME
- ○ COOK / EAT A HEALTHY MEAL
- ○ ORGANIZE MY SPACE / LIFE
- ○ GET RID OF THINGS I DON'T LOVE
- ○ BE WITH FRIENDS
- ○ PLAY
- ○ LET GO / FORGIVE
- ○ SING / MAKE MUSIC
- ○ CREATE ART
- ○ READ FOR ENJOYMENT
- ○ CONNECT / PRAY
- ○ CALL SOMEONE / WRITE A LETTER
- ○ STRETCH / DO YOGA
- ○ MASSAGE / EXCHANGE TOUCH
- ○ SERVE MY COMMUNITY

DREAM, EXPAND, RECORD, REFLECT:

Rituals for Living Challenge

This week, cook at least four nice meals. Infuse the food with love. If you already cook regularly, challenge yourself in another way – cook something really special, cook a meal you'd usually not cook, or cook for someone else.

TOP 3 GOALS THIS WEEK

TASKS
- MONTHLY PLAN
- INCOMPLETE FROM LAST WEEK
- LIFE DUTIES
- ★ STAR THE MOST IMPORTANT TASKS ★

Final task: schedule next week

NOW: PUT THESE TASKS & RITUALS IN YOUR CALENDAR, GO FORTH AND CONQUER!

MONTH:

	MONDAY	TUESDAY	WEDNESDAY
	INTENTION:	INTENTION:	INTENTION:
	MORNING RITUALS AND ACTIVITIES	MORNING RITUALS AND ACTIVITIES	MORNING RITUALS AND ACTIVITIES
8:00			
8:30			
9:00			
9:30			
10:00			
10:30			
11:00			
11:30			
	WHAT SHALL I BE FOCUSED ON?	WHERE IS MY ATTENTION GOING?	WHAT PERSPECTIVE DO I CHOOSE?
12:00			
12:30			
1:00			
1:30			
2:00			
2:30			
3:00			
3:30			
4:00			
4:30			
5:00			
5:30			
6:00			
	EVENING RITUALS AND ACTIVITIES	EVENING RITUALS AND ACTIVITIES	EVENING RITUALS AND ACTIVITIES
	I AM GRATEFUL FOR:	I AM GRATEFUL FOR:	I AM GRATEFUL FOR:

RITUALS FOR THRIVING

- ○ EXERCISE
- ○ MEDITATE / BREATHE
- ○ JOURNAL
- ○ DANCE
- ○ GO ON A DATE
- ○ CONNECT WITH NATURE
- ○ VISUALIZE
- ○ FAMILY TIME
- ○ COOK / EAT A HEALTHY MEAL
- ○ ORGANIZE MY SPACE / LIFE
- ○ GET RID OF THINGS I DON'T LOVE
- ○ BE WITH FRIENDS
- ○ PLAY
- ○ LET GO / FORGIVE
- ○ SING / MAKE MUSIC
- ○ CREATE ART
- ○ READ FOR ENJOYMENT
- ○ CONNECT / PRAY
- ○ CALL SOMEONE / WRITE A LETTER
- ○ STRETCH / DO YOGA
- ○ MASSAGE / EXCHANGE TOUCH
- ○ SERVE MY COMMUNITY

	THURSDAY	FRIDAY	SATURDAY
	INTENTION:	INTENTION:	INTENTION:
	MORNING RITUALS AND ACTIVITIES	MORNING RITUALS AND ACTIVITIES	MORNING RITUALS AND ACTIVITIES
8:00			
8:30			
9:00			
9:30			EVENING RITUALS AND ACTIVITIES
10:00			
10:30			
11:00			
11:30			I AM GRATEFUL FOR:
	HOW AM I SPENDING MY ENERGY?	HOW DO I AFFECT MY WORLD?	
12:00			
12:30			
1:00			
1:30			
2:00			SUNDAY
2:30			INTENTION:
3:00			
3:30			
4:00			MORNING RITUALS AND ACTIVITIES
4:30			
5:00			
5:30			
6:00			
	EVENING RITUALS AND ACTIVITIES	EVENING RITUALS AND ACTIVITIES	
			EVENING RITUALS AND ACTIVITIES
	I AM GRATEFUL FOR:	I AM GRATEFUL FOR:	
			I AM GRATEFUL FOR:

DREAM, EXPAND, RECORD, REFLECT:

FOCUS

Rituals for Living Challenge
This week, light a candle at every meal – or at least for one meal – each day.
If you like, let it remind you of the power of the sun and the gift of life that made this meal possible, or a special presence you'd like to invite to the meal.

TOP 3 GOALS THIS WEEK

TASKS
- MONTHLY PLAN
- INCOMPLETE FROM LAST WEEK
- LIFE DUTIES
- ★ STAR THE MOST IMPORTANT TASKS ★

Final task: schedule next week
NOW: PUT THESE TASKS & RITUALS IN YOUR CALENDAR, GO FORTH AND CONQUER!

MONTH:

	MONDAY	TUESDAY	WEDNESDAY
	INTENTION:	INTENTION:	INTENTION:
	MORNING RITUALS AND ACTIVITIES	MORNING RITUALS AND ACTIVITIES	MORNING RITUALS AND ACTIVITIES
8:00			
8:30			
9:00			
9:30			
10:00			
10:30			
11:00			
11:30			
	WHAT SHALL I BE FOCUSED ON?	WHERE IS MY ATTENTION GOING?	WHAT PERSPECTIVE DO I CHOOSE?
12:00			
12:30			
1:00			
1:30			
2:00			
2:30			
3:00			
3:30			
4:00			
4:30			
5:00			
5:30			
6:00			
	EVENING RITUALS AND ACTIVITIES	EVENING RITUALS AND ACTIVITIES	EVENING RITUALS AND ACTIVITIES
	I AM GRATEFUL FOR:	I AM GRATEFUL FOR:	I AM GRATEFUL FOR:

RITUALS FOR THRIVING

- ○ EXERCISE
- ○ MEDITATE / BREATHE
- ○ JOURNAL
- ○ DANCE
- ○ GO ON A DATE
- ○ CONNECT WITH NATURE
- ○ VISUALIZE
- ○ FAMILY TIME
- ○ COOK / EAT A HEALTHY MEAL
- ○ ORGANIZE MY SPACE / LIFE
- ○ GET RID OF THINGS I DON'T LOVE
- ○ BE WITH FRIENDS
- ○ PLAY
- ○ LET GO / FORGIVE
- ○ SING / MAKE MUSIC
- ○ CREATE ART
- ○ READ FOR ENJOYMENT
- ○ CONNECT / PRAY
- ○ CALL SOMEONE / WRITE A LETTER
- ○ STRETCH / DO YOGA
- ○ MASSAGE / EXCHANGE TOUCH
- ○ SERVE MY COMMUNITY

THURSDAY	FRIDAY	SATURDAY
INTENTION:	INTENTION:	INTENTION:
MORNING RITUALS AND ACTIVITIES	MORNING RITUALS AND ACTIVITIES	MORNING RITUALS AND ACTIVITIES
8:00	8:00	
8:30	8:30	
9:00	9:00	
9:30	9:30	EVENING RITUALS AND ACTIVITIES
10:00	10:00	
10:30	10:30	
11:00	11:00	
11:30	11:30	I AM GRATEFUL FOR:
HOW AM I SPENDING MY ENERGY?	HOW DO I AFFECT MY WORLD?	
12:00	12:00	
12:30	12:30	
1:00	1:00	
1:30	1:30	
2:00	2:00	SUNDAY
2:30	2:30	INTENTION:
3:00	3:00	
3:30	3:30	
4:00	4:00	MORNING RITUALS AND ACTIVITIES
4:30	4:30	
5:00	5:00	
5:30	5:30	
6:00	6:00	
EVENING RITUALS AND ACTIVITIES	EVENING RITUALS AND ACTIVITIES	
		EVENING RITUALS AND ACTIVITIES
I AM GRATEFUL FOR:	I AM GRATEFUL FOR:	
		I AM GRATEFUL FOR:

DREAM, EXPAND, RECORD, REFLECT:

FOCUS

Rituals for Living Challenge
This week, exercise to the point of breaking a sweat at least 4 times. If you are exhausted or have been chronically ill, instead use this week to learn your limits. Move your body daily, but never to the point that it leaves you more tired.

TOP 3 GOALS THIS WEEK

TASKS
- MONTHLY PLAN
- INCOMPLETE FROM LAST WEEK
- LIFE DUTIES
- ★ STAR THE MOST IMPORTANT TASKS ★

Final task: schedule next week

NOW: PUT THESE TASKS & RITUALS IN YOUR CALENDAR, GO FORTH AND CONQUER!

MONTH:

	MONDAY	TUESDAY	WEDNESDAY
	INTENTION:	INTENTION:	INTENTION:
	MORNING RITUALS AND ACTIVITIES	MORNING RITUALS AND ACTIVITIES	MORNING RITUALS AND ACTIVITIES
8:00			
8:30			
9:00			
9:30			
10:00			
10:30			
11:00			
11:30			
	WHAT SHALL I BE FOCUSED ON?	WHERE IS MY ATTENTION GOING?	WHAT PERSPECTIVE DO I CHOOSE?
12:00			
12:30			
1:00			
1:30			
2:00			
2:30			
3:00			
3:30			
4:00			
4:30			
5:00			
5:30			
6:00			
	EVENING RITUALS AND ACTIVITIES	EVENING RITUALS AND ACTIVITIES	EVENING RITUALS AND ACTIVITIES
	I AM GRATEFUL FOR:	I AM GRATEFUL FOR:	I AM GRATEFUL FOR:

RITUALS FOR THRIVING

- ○ EXERCISE
- ○ MEDITATE / BREATHE
- ○ JOURNAL
- ○ DANCE
- ○ GO ON A DATE
- ○ CONNECT WITH NATURE
- ○ VISUALIZE
- ○ FAMILY TIME
- ○ COOK / EAT A HEALTHY MEAL
- ○ ORGANIZE MY SPACE / LIFE
- ○ GET RID OF THINGS I DON'T LOVE
- ○ BE WITH FRIENDS
- ○ PLAY
- ○ LET GO / FORGIVE
- ○ SING / MAKE MUSIC
- ○ CREATE ART
- ○ READ FOR ENJOYMENT
- ○ CONNECT / PRAY
- ○ CALL SOMEONE / WRITE A LETTER
- ○ STRETCH / DO YOGA
- ○ MASSAGE / EXCHANGE TOUCH
- ○ SERVE MY COMMUNITY

THURSDAY	FRIDAY	SATURDAY
INTENTION:	INTENTION:	INTENTION:
MORNING RITUALS AND ACTIVITIES	MORNING RITUALS AND ACTIVITIES	MORNING RITUALS AND ACTIVITIES
8:00	8:00	
8:30	8:30	
9:00	9:00	
9:30	9:30	EVENING RITUALS AND ACTIVITIES
10:00	10:00	
10:30	10:30	
11:00	11:00	
11:30	11:30	I AM GRATEFUL FOR:
HOW AM I SPENDING MY ENERGY?	HOW DO I AFFECT MY WORLD?	
12:00	12:00	
12:30	12:30	
1:00	1:00	
1:30	1:30	
2:00	2:00	**SUNDAY**
2:30	2:30	INTENTION:
3:00	3:00	
3:30	3:30	
4:00	4:00	MORNING RITUALS AND ACTIVITIES
4:30	4:30	
5:00	5:00	
5:30	5:30	
6:00	6:00	
EVENING RITUALS AND ACTIVITIES	EVENING RITUALS AND ACTIVITIES	
		EVENING RITUALS AND ACTIVITIES
I AM GRATEFUL FOR:	I AM GRATEFUL FOR:	
		I AM GRATEFUL FOR:

DREAM, EXPAND, RECORD, REFLECT:

Rituals for Living Challenge

This week, as often as possible, make a conscious decision to feel LIGHT. Lightness is always available, even when things seem dark or heavy.
You can always choose to be light.

TOP 3 GOALS THIS WEEK

TASKS
- MONTHLY PLAN
- INCOMPLETE FROM LAST WEEK
- LIFE DUTIES
- ★ STAR THE MOST IMPORTANT TASKS ★

Final task: schedule next week

NOW: PUT THESE TASKS & RITUALS IN YOUR CALENDAR, GO FORTH AND CONQUER!

MONTH:

	MONDAY	TUESDAY	WEDNESDAY
	INTENTION:	INTENTION:	INTENTION:
	MORNING RITUALS AND ACTIVITIES	MORNING RITUALS AND ACTIVITIES	MORNING RITUALS AND ACTIVITIES
8:00			
8:30			
9:00			
9:30			
10:00			
10:30			
11:00			
11:30			
	WHAT SHALL I BE FOCUSED ON?	WHERE IS MY ATTENTION GOING?	WHAT PERSPECTIVE DO I CHOOSE?
12:00			
12:30			
1:00			
1:30			
2:00			
2:30			
3:00			
3:30			
4:00			
4:30			
5:00			
5:30			
6:00			
	EVENING RITUALS AND ACTIVITIES	EVENING RITUALS AND ACTIVITIES	EVENING RITUALS AND ACTIVITIES
	I AM GRATEFUL FOR:	I AM GRATEFUL FOR:	I AM GRATEFUL FOR:

RITUALS FOR THRIVING

- ○ EXERCISE
- ○ MEDITATE / BREATHE
- ○ JOURNAL
- ○ DANCE
- ○ GO ON A DATE
- ○ CONNECT WITH NATURE
- ○ VISUALIZE
- ○ FAMILY TIME
- ○ COOK / EAT A HEALTHY MEAL
- ○ ORGANIZE MY SPACE / LIFE
- ○ GET RID OF THINGS I DON'T LOVE
- ○ BE WITH FRIENDS
- ○ PLAY
- ○ LET GO / FORGIVE
- ○ SING / MAKE MUSIC
- ○ CREATE ART
- ○ READ FOR ENJOYMENT
- ○ CONNECT / PRAY
- ○ CALL SOMEONE / WRITE A LETTER
- ○ STRETCH / DO YOGA
- ○ MASSAGE / EXCHANGE TOUCH
- ○ SERVE MY COMMUNITY

THURSDAY	FRIDAY	SATURDAY
INTENTION:	INTENTION:	INTENTION:
MORNING RITUALS AND ACTIVITIES	MORNING RITUALS AND ACTIVITIES	MORNING RITUALS AND ACTIVITIES
8:00	8:00	
8:30	8:30	
9:00	9:00	
9:30	9:30	EVENING RITUALS AND ACTIVITIES
10:00	10:00	
10:30	10:30	
11:00	11:00	
11:30	11:30	I AM GRATEFUL FOR:
HOW AM I SPENDING MY ENERGY?	HOW DO I AFFECT MY WORLD?	
12:00	12:00	
12:30	12:30	
1:00	1:00	
1:30	1:30	
2:00	2:00	SUNDAY
2:30	2:30	INTENTION:
3:00	3:00	
3:30	3:30	
4:00	4:00	MORNING RITUALS AND ACTIVITIES
4:30	4:30	
5:00	5:00	
5:30	5:30	
6:00	6:00	
EVENING RITUALS AND ACTIVITIES	EVENING RITUALS AND ACTIVITIES	
		EVENING RITUALS AND ACTIVITIES
I AM GRATEFUL FOR:	I AM GRATEFUL FOR:	
		I AM GRATEFUL FOR:

DREAM, EXPAND, RECORD, REFLECT:

Rituals for Living Challenge

This week, engage in some form of play – real play, in which you ideally abandon your self-consciousness and let loose – on at least four days.

TOP 3 GOALS THIS WEEK

TASKS
- MONTHLY PLAN
- INCOMPLETE FROM LAST WEEK
- LIFE DUTIES
- ★ STAR THE MOST IMPORTANT TASKS ★

Final task: schedule next week

NOW: PUT THESE TASKS & RITUALS IN YOUR CALENDAR, GO FORTH AND CONQUER!

MONTH:

	MONDAY	TUESDAY	WEDNESDAY
	INTENTION:	INTENTION:	INTENTION:
	MORNING RITUALS AND ACTIVITIES	MORNING RITUALS AND ACTIVITIES	MORNING RITUALS AND ACTIVITIES
8:00			
8:30			
9:00			
9:30			
10:00			
10:30			
11:00			
11:30			
	WHAT SHALL I BE FOCUSED ON?	WHERE IS MY ATTENTION GOING?	WHAT PERSPECTIVE DO I CHOOSE?
12:00			
12:30			
1:00			
1:30			
2:00			
2:30			
3:00			
3:30			
4:00			
4:30			
5:00			
5:30			
6:00			
	EVENING RITUALS AND ACTIVITIES	EVENING RITUALS AND ACTIVITIES	EVENING RITUALS AND ACTIVITIES
	I AM GRATEFUL FOR:	I AM GRATEFUL FOR:	I AM GRATEFUL FOR:

RITUALS FOR THRIVING

- ○ EXERCISE
- ○ MEDITATE / BREATHE
- ○ JOURNAL
- ○ DANCE
- ○ GO ON A DATE
- ○ CONNECT WITH NATURE
- ○ VISUALIZE
- ○ FAMILY TIME
- ○ COOK / EAT A HEALTHY MEAL
- ○ ORGANIZE MY SPACE / LIFE
- ○ GET RID OF THINGS I DON'T LOVE
- ○ BE WITH FRIENDS
- ○ PLAY
- ○ LET GO / FORGIVE
- ○ SING / MAKE MUSIC
- ○ CREATE ART
- ○ READ FOR ENJOYMENT
- ○ CONNECT / PRAY
- ○ CALL SOMEONE / WRITE A LETTER
- ○ STRETCH / DO YOGA
- ○ MASSAGE / EXCHANGE TOUCH
- ○ SERVE MY COMMUNITY

THURSDAY	FRIDAY	SATURDAY
INTENTION:	INTENTION:	INTENTION:
MORNING RITUALS AND ACTIVITIES	MORNING RITUALS AND ACTIVITIES	MORNING RITUALS AND ACTIVITIES
8:00	8:00	
8:30	8:30	
9:00	9:00	
9:30	9:30	EVENING RITUALS AND ACTIVITIES
10:00	10:00	
10:30	10:30	
11:00	11:00	
11:30	11:30	I AM GRATEFUL FOR:
HOW AM I SPENDING MY ENERGY?	HOW DO I AFFECT MY WORLD?	
12:00	12:00	
12:30	12:30	
1:00	1:00	
1:30	1:30	
2:00	2:00	**SUNDAY**
2:30	2:30	INTENTION:
3:00	3:00	
3:30	3:30	
4:00	4:00	MORNING RITUALS AND ACTIVITIES
4:30	4:30	
5:00	5:00	
5:30	5:30	
6:00	6:00	
EVENING RITUALS AND ACTIVITIES	EVENING RITUALS AND ACTIVITIES	
		EVENING RITUALS AND ACTIVITIES
I AM GRATEFUL FOR:	I AM GRATEFUL FOR:	
		I AM GRATEFUL FOR:

DREAM, EXPAND, RECORD, REFLECT:

Rituals for Living Challenge

This week, every time you wash yourself (hands, body, etc.), set an intention of washing away something you'd like to let go of that you've been holding onto, or intend for the water to purify or nourish some part of yourself.

TOP 3 GOALS THIS WEEK

TASKS
- MONTHLY PLAN
- INCOMPLETE FROM LAST WEEK
- LIFE DUTIES
- ★ STAR THE MOST IMPORTANT TASKS ★

Final task: schedule next week

NOW: PUT THESE TASKS & RITUALS IN YOUR CALENDAR, GO FORTH AND CONQUER!

MONTH:

	MONDAY	TUESDAY	WEDNESDAY
	INTENTION:	INTENTION:	INTENTION:
	MORNING RITUALS AND ACTIVITIES	MORNING RITUALS AND ACTIVITIES	MORNING RITUALS AND ACTIVITIES
8:00			
8:30			
9:00			
9:30			
10:00			
10:30			
11:00			
11:30			
	WHAT SHALL I BE FOCUSED ON?	WHERE IS MY ATTENTION GOING?	WHAT PERSPECTIVE DO I CHOOSE?
12:00			
12:30			
1:00			
1:30			
2:00			
2:30			
3:00			
3:30			
4:00			
4:30			
5:00			
5:30			
6:00			
	EVENING RITUALS AND ACTIVITIES	EVENING RITUALS AND ACTIVITIES	EVENING RITUALS AND ACTIVITIES
	I AM GRATEFUL FOR:	I AM GRATEFUL FOR:	I AM GRATEFUL FOR:

THURSDAY	FRIDAY	SATURDAY	RITUALS FOR THRIVING
INTENTION:	INTENTION:	INTENTION:	○ EXERCISE
			○ MEDITATE / BREATHE
			○ JOURNAL
			○ DANCE
			○ GO ON A DATE
MORNING RITUALS AND ACTIVITIES	MORNING RITUALS AND ACTIVITIES	MORNING RITUALS AND ACTIVITIES	○ CONNECT WITH NATURE
			○ VISUALIZE
			○ FAMILY TIME
			○ COOK / EAT A HEALTHY MEAL
			○ ORGANIZE MY SPACE / LIFE
8:00	8:00		○ GET RID OF THINGS I DON'T LOVE
8:30	8:30		○ BE WITH FRIENDS
9:00	9:00		○ PLAY
9:30	9:30	EVENING RITUALS AND ACTIVITIES	○ LET GO / FORGIVE
10:00	10:00		○ SING / MAKE MUSIC
10:30	10:30		○ CREATE ART
11:00	11:00		○ READ FOR ENJOYMENT
11:30	11:30	I AM GRATEFUL FOR:	○ CONNECT / PRAY
HOW AM I SPENDING MY ENERGY?	HOW DO I AFFECT MY WORLD?		○ CALL SOMEONE / WRITE A LETTER
12:00	12:00		○ STRETCH / DO YOGA
12:30	12:30		○ MASSAGE / EXCHANGE TOUCH
1:00	1:00		○ SERVE MY COMMUNITY
1:30	1:30		
2:00	2:00	SUNDAY	DREAM, EXPAND, RECORD, REFLECT:
2:30	2:30	INTENTION:	
3:00	3:00		
3:30	3:30		
4:00	4:00	MORNING RITUALS AND ACTIVITIES	
4:30	4:30		
5:00	5:00		
5:30	5:30		
6:00	6:00		
EVENING RITUALS AND ACTIVITIES	EVENING RITUALS AND ACTIVITIES		
		EVENING RITUALS AND ACTIVITIES	
I AM GRATEFUL FOR:	I AM GRATEFUL FOR:		
		I AM GRATEFUL FOR:	

FOCUS

Rituals for Living Challenge
Try dry skin brushing at least 3 times. Get a natural skin brush, undress, and vigorously brush every inch of your skin, stroking always toward your heart. Start at your toes and work up. Then fingers to heart. Then torso. (More info online)

TOP 3 GOALS THIS WEEK

TASKS
- MONTHLY PLAN
- INCOMPLETE FROM LAST WEEK
- LIFE DUTIES
- ★ STAR THE MOST IMPORTANT TASKS ★

Final task: schedule next week

NOW: PUT THESE TASKS & RITUALS IN YOUR CALENDAR, GO FORTH AND CONQUER!

MONTH:

	MONDAY	TUESDAY	WEDNESDAY
	INTENTION:	INTENTION:	INTENTION:
	MORNING RITUALS AND ACTIVITIES	MORNING RITUALS AND ACTIVITIES	MORNING RITUALS AND ACTIVITIES
8:00			
8:30			
9:00			
9:30			
10:00			
10:30			
11:00			
11:30			
	WHAT SHALL I BE FOCUSED ON?	WHERE IS MY ATTENTION GOING?	WHAT PERSPECTIVE DO I CHOOSE?
12:00			
12:30			
1:00			
1:30			
2:00			
2:30			
3:00			
3:30			
4:00			
4:30			
5:00			
5:30			
6:00			
	EVENING RITUALS AND ACTIVITIES	EVENING RITUALS AND ACTIVITIES	EVENING RITUALS AND ACTIVITIES
	I AM GRATEFUL FOR:	I AM GRATEFUL FOR:	I AM GRATEFUL FOR:

THURSDAY	FRIDAY	SATURDAY
INTENTION:	INTENTION:	INTENTION:
MORNING RITUALS AND ACTIVITIES	MORNING RITUALS AND ACTIVITIES	MORNING RITUALS AND ACTIVITIES
8:00	8:00	
8:30	8:30	
9:00	9:00	
9:30	9:30	EVENING RITUALS AND ACTIVITIES
10:00	10:00	
10:30	10:30	
11:00	11:00	
11:30	11:30	I AM GRATEFUL FOR:
HOW AM I SPENDING MY ENERGY?	HOW DO I AFFECT MY WORLD?	
12:00	12:00	
12:30	12:30	
1:00	1:00	
1:30	1:30	
2:00	2:00	SUNDAY
2:30	2:30	INTENTION:
3:00	3:00	
3:30	3:30	
4:00	4:00	MORNING RITUALS AND ACTIVITIES
4:30	4:30	
5:00	5:00	
5:30	5:30	
6:00	6:00	
EVENING RITUALS AND ACTIVITIES	EVENING RITUALS AND ACTIVITIES	
		EVENING RITUALS AND ACTIVITIES
I AM GRATEFUL FOR:	I AM GRATEFUL FOR:	
		I AM GRATEFUL FOR:

RITUALS FOR THRIVING

- ○ EXERCISE
- ○ MEDITATE / BREATHE
- ○ JOURNAL
- ○ DANCE
- ○ GO ON A DATE
- ○ CONNECT WITH NATURE
- ○ VISUALIZE
- ○ FAMILY TIME
- ○ COOK / EAT A HEALTHY MEAL
- ○ ORGANIZE MY SPACE / LIFE
- ○ GET RID OF THINGS I DON'T LOVE
- ○ BE WITH FRIENDS
- ○ PLAY
- ○ LET GO / FORGIVE
- ○ SING / MAKE MUSIC
- ○ CREATE ART
- ○ READ FOR ENJOYMENT
- ○ CONNECT / PRAY
- ○ CALL SOMEONE / WRITE A LETTER
- ○ STRETCH / DO YOGA
- ○ MASSAGE / EXCHANGE TOUCH
- ○ SERVE MY COMMUNITY

DREAM, EXPAND, RECORD, REFLECT:

Rituals for Living Challenge

This week, get flexible. Stretch for at least ten minutes each day. Breathe into each part as you meet resistance & allow it to open. Meanwhile, stretch your mind. Be more flexible and open with your opinions, beliefs, and judgments.

TOP 3 GOALS THIS WEEK

TASKS
- MONTHLY PLAN
- INCOMPLETE FROM LAST WEEK
- LIFE DUTIES
- ★ STAR THE MOST IMPORTANT TASKS ★

Final task: schedule next week

NOW: PUT THESE TASKS & RITUALS IN YOUR CALENDAR, GO FORTH AND CONQUER!

MONTH:

	MONDAY	TUESDAY	WEDNESDAY
	INTENTION:	INTENTION:	INTENTION:
	MORNING RITUALS AND ACTIVITIES	MORNING RITUALS AND ACTIVITIES	MORNING RITUALS AND ACTIVITIES
8:00			
8:30			
9:00			
9:30			
10:00			
10:30			
11:00			
11:30			
	WHAT SHALL I BE FOCUSED ON?	WHERE IS MY ATTENTION GOING?	WHAT PERSPECTIVE DO I CHOOSE?
12:00			
12:30			
1:00			
1:30			
2:00			
2:30			
3:00			
3:30			
4:00			
4:30			
5:00			
5:30			
6:00			
	EVENING RITUALS AND ACTIVITIES	EVENING RITUALS AND ACTIVITIES	EVENING RITUALS AND ACTIVITIES
	I AM GRATEFUL FOR:	I AM GRATEFUL FOR:	I AM GRATEFUL FOR:

RITUALS FOR THRIVING

- ○ EXERCISE
- ○ MEDITATE / BREATHE
- ○ JOURNAL
- ○ DANCE
- ○ GO ON A DATE
- ○ CONNECT WITH NATURE
- ○ VISUALIZE
- ○ FAMILY TIME
- ○ COOK / EAT A HEALTHY MEAL
- ○ ORGANIZE MY SPACE / LIFE
- ○ GET RID OF THINGS I DON'T LOVE
- ○ BE WITH FRIENDS
- ○ PLAY
- ○ LET GO / FORGIVE
- ○ SING / MAKE MUSIC
- ○ CREATE ART
- ○ READ FOR ENJOYMENT
- ○ CONNECT / PRAY
- ○ CALL SOMEONE / WRITE A LETTER
- ○ STRETCH / DO YOGA
- ○ MASSAGE / EXCHANGE TOUCH
- ○ SERVE MY COMMUNITY

THURSDAY	FRIDAY	SATURDAY
INTENTION:	INTENTION:	INTENTION:
MORNING RITUALS AND ACTIVITIES	MORNING RITUALS AND ACTIVITIES	MORNING RITUALS AND ACTIVITIES
8:00	8:00	
8:30	8:30	
9:00	9:00	
9:30	9:30	EVENING RITUALS AND ACTIVITIES
10:00	10:00	
10:30	10:30	
11:00	11:00	
11:30	11:30	I AM GRATEFUL FOR:
HOW AM I SPENDING MY ENERGY?	HOW DO I AFFECT MY WORLD?	
12:00	12:00	
12:30	12:30	
1:00	1:00	
1:30	1:30	
2:00	2:00	**SUNDAY**
2:30	2:30	INTENTION:
3:00	3:00	
3:30	3:30	
4:00	4:00	MORNING RITUALS AND ACTIVITIES
4:30	4:30	
5:00	5:00	
5:30	5:30	
6:00	6:00	
EVENING RITUALS AND ACTIVITIES	EVENING RITUALS AND ACTIVITIES	
		EVENING RITUALS AND ACTIVITIES
I AM GRATEFUL FOR:	I AM GRATEFUL FOR:	
		I AM GRATEFUL FOR:

DREAM, EXPAND, RECORD, REFLECT:

FOCUS

Rituals for Living Challenge

This week, be fascinated. Notice all the tiny details and intricacy. The brilliance in every creation, both natural and manmade. See the profound beauty and design in every pebble, eye, or pen. Tune in, wake up, be fascinated.

TOP 3 GOALS THIS WEEK

TASKS
- MONTHLY PLAN
- INCOMPLETE FROM LAST WEEK
- LIFE DUTIES
- ★ STAR THE MOST IMPORTANT TASKS ★

Final task: schedule next week

NOW: PUT THESE TASKS & RITUALS IN YOUR CALENDAR, GO FORTH AND CONQUER!

MONTH:

	MONDAY	TUESDAY	WEDNESDAY
	INTENTION:	INTENTION:	INTENTION:
	MORNING RITUALS AND ACTIVITIES	MORNING RITUALS AND ACTIVITIES	MORNING RITUALS AND ACTIVITIES
8:00			
8:30			
9:00			
9:30			
10:00			
10:30			
11:00			
11:30			
	WHAT SHALL I BE FOCUSED ON?	WHERE IS MY ATTENTION GOING?	WHAT PERSPECTIVE DO I CHOOSE?
12:00			
12:30			
1:00			
1:30			
2:00			
2:30			
3:00			
3:30			
4:00			
4:30			
5:00			
5:30			
6:00			
	EVENING RITUALS AND ACTIVITIES	EVENING RITUALS AND ACTIVITIES	EVENING RITUALS AND ACTIVITIES
	I AM GRATEFUL FOR:	I AM GRATEFUL FOR:	I AM GRATEFUL FOR:

THURSDAY	FRIDAY	SATURDAY
INTENTION:	INTENTION:	INTENTION:
MORNING RITUALS AND ACTIVITIES	MORNING RITUALS AND ACTIVITIES	MORNING RITUALS AND ACTIVITIES
8:00	8:00	
8:30	8:30	
9:00	9:00	
9:30	9:30	EVENING RITUALS AND ACTIVITIES
10:00	10:00	
10:30	10:30	
11:00	11:00	
11:30	11:30	I AM GRATEFUL FOR:
HOW AM I SPENDING MY ENERGY?	HOW DO I AFFECT MY WORLD?	
12:00	12:00	
12:30	12:30	
1:00	1:00	
1:30	1:30	
2:00	2:00	SUNDAY
2:30	2:30	INTENTION:
3:00	3:00	
3:30	3:30	
4:00	4:00	MORNING RITUALS AND ACTIVITIES
4:30	4:30	
5:00	5:00	
5:30	5:30	
6:00	6:00	
EVENING RITUALS AND ACTIVITIES	EVENING RITUALS AND ACTIVITIES	
		EVENING RITUALS AND ACTIVITIES
I AM GRATEFUL FOR:	I AM GRATEFUL FOR:	
		I AM GRATEFUL FOR:

RITUALS FOR THRIVING

- ○ EXERCISE
- ○ MEDITATE / BREATHE
- ○ JOURNAL
- ○ DANCE
- ○ GO ON A DATE
- ○ CONNECT WITH NATURE
- ○ VISUALIZE
- ○ FAMILY TIME
- ○ COOK / EAT A HEALTHY MEAL
- ○ ORGANIZE MY SPACE / LIFE
- ○ GET RID OF THINGS I DON'T LOVE
- ○ BE WITH FRIENDS
- ○ PLAY
- ○ LET GO / FORGIVE
- ○ SING / MAKE MUSIC
- ○ CREATE ART
- ○ READ FOR ENJOYMENT
- ○ CONNECT / PRAY
- ○ CALL SOMEONE / WRITE A LETTER
- ○ STRETCH / DO YOGA
- ○ MASSAGE / EXCHANGE TOUCH
- ○ SERVE MY COMMUNITY

DREAM, EXPAND, RECORD, REFLECT:

Rituals for Living Challenge

The week of eye contact: make eye contact with everyone you meet. As you do, relax in your body. What happens if you make a mental communication while holding their gaze, such as, "I'm here for you" or "I love you"? Soul windows.

TOP 3 GOALS THIS WEEK

TASKS
- MONTHLY PLAN
- INCOMPLETE FROM LAST WEEK
- LIFE DUTIES
- ★ STAR THE MOST IMPORTANT TASKS ★

Final task: schedule next week

NOW: PUT THESE TASKS & RITUALS IN YOUR CALENDAR, GO FORTH AND CONQUER!

MONTH:

	MONDAY	TUESDAY	WEDNESDAY
	INTENTION:	**INTENTION:**	**INTENTION:**
	MORNING RITUALS AND ACTIVITIES	**MORNING RITUALS AND ACTIVITIES**	**MORNING RITUALS AND ACTIVITIES**
8:00			
8:30			
9:00			
9:30			
10:00			
10:30			
11:00			
11:30			
	WHAT SHALL I BE FOCUSED ON?	**WHERE IS MY ATTENTION GOING?**	**WHAT PERSPECTIVE DO I CHOOSE?**
12:00			
12:30			
1:00			
1:30			
2:00			
2:30			
3:00			
3:30			
4:00			
4:30			
5:00			
5:30			
6:00			
	EVENING RITUALS AND ACTIVITIES	**EVENING RITUALS AND ACTIVITIES**	**EVENING RITUALS AND ACTIVITIES**
	I AM GRATEFUL FOR:	**I AM GRATEFUL FOR:**	**I AM GRATEFUL FOR:**

THURSDAY	FRIDAY	SATURDAY
INTENTION:	INTENTION:	INTENTION:
MORNING RITUALS AND ACTIVITIES	MORNING RITUALS AND ACTIVITIES	MORNING RITUALS AND ACTIVITIES
8:00	8:00	
8:30	8:30	
9:00	9:00	
9:30	9:30	EVENING RITUALS AND ACTIVITIES
10:00	10:00	
10:30	10:30	
11:00	11:00	
11:30	11:30	I AM GRATEFUL FOR:
HOW AM I SPENDING MY ENERGY?	HOW DO I AFFECT MY WORLD?	
12:00	12:00	
12:30	12:30	
1:00	1:00	
1:30	1:30	
2:00	2:00	SUNDAY
2:30	2:30	INTENTION:
3:00	3:00	
3:30	3:30	
4:00	4:00	MORNING RITUALS AND ACTIVITIES
4:30	4:30	
5:00	5:00	
5:30	5:30	
6:00	6:00	
EVENING RITUALS AND ACTIVITIES	EVENING RITUALS AND ACTIVITIES	
		EVENING RITUALS AND ACTIVITIES
I AM GRATEFUL FOR:	I AM GRATEFUL FOR:	
		I AM GRATEFUL FOR:

RITUALS FOR THRIVING

- ○ EXERCISE
- ○ MEDITATE / BREATHE
- ○ JOURNAL
- ○ DANCE
- ○ GO ON A DATE
- ○ CONNECT WITH NATURE
- ○ VISUALIZE
- ○ FAMILY TIME
- ○ COOK / EAT A HEALTHY MEAL
- ○ ORGANIZE MY SPACE / LIFE
- ○ GET RID OF THINGS I DON'T LOVE
- ○ BE WITH FRIENDS
- ○ PLAY
- ○ LET GO / FORGIVE
- ○ SING / MAKE MUSIC
- ○ CREATE ART
- ○ READ FOR ENJOYMENT
- ○ CONNECT / PRAY
- ○ CALL SOMEONE / WRITE A LETTER
- ○ STRETCH / DO YOGA
- ○ MASSAGE / EXCHANGE TOUCH
- ○ SERVE MY COMMUNITY

DREAM, EXPAND, RECORD, REFLECT:

Reflect

Improvement is possible only through our capacity to reflect.

What were the most memorable moments of the past year?

_____
_____
_____
_____
_____
_____
_____
_____

What were your biggest challenges of the past year?

_____
_____
_____
_____
_____
_____
_____
_____

How did you *ritualize* your goals, your health, and your happiness, and in what ways did this affect you?

_____
_____
_____
_____
_____
_____
_____
_____

What worked? What did you achieve over the past year?

___

What didn't work? How might you do things differently in the future?

___

What were the best lessons you learned?

___

What was your theme for the past year? How did the year pan out with regard to this theme?

___

Someday Maybe List

ideas that may or may not turn out to be worth pursuing

Items to Add to Next Year's Plan

ideas that are <u>definitely</u> worth pursuing

For over a decade, our slogan has been "A peaceful world begins with a peaceful you."

And although peaceful individuals are the foundation of a peaceful world,

when it comes to initiating real change in a profound way,

we need people who are not just peaceful, but also powerful.

Individuals who have aligned their hearts with their ambitions.

Individuals who are dreaming *and* doing.

Individuals like you.

Thank you for making the world more awesome.

Love,

Briana and Peter

PRINTED IN THE USA